MARITAL SECRETS
FOR A
SUCCESSFUL
MARRIAGE

CHARLES SOYOYE

Printed in the United States of America

Library of Congress Control Number: 2019916907
ISBN:Softcover   978-1-64376-500-6
eBook   978-1-64376-499-3

Republished by: PageTurner, Press and Media LLC
Publication Date: November 14, 2019

To order copies of this book, contact:

PageTurner, Press and Media
Phone: 1-888-447-9651
order@pageturner.us
www.pageturner.us

To my darling wife and my great companion,

Mrs. Oladunni Soyoye.

I love and appreciate you everyday and in many ways. I thank God for your life and for being my wife and the mother of our children for the past 29 years. Thank you.

May God continues to bless you with good health, long life, peace of mind and joy in Jesus Christ name.

Amen.

Marriage involves the public act of leaving – making a lifelong commitment to your partner that takes priority even over your parental relationships. *"That is why a man leaves his father and mother and is joined to his wife. In this way two people become one"*. (Genesis 2:24) ERV.

I believe that you can have the Agape love for your spouse. The love that is selfless that God wants you to have that is not just emotional, but the conscious act of the will, that is a deliberate decision on your part to put your spouse ahead of yourself. This is the kind of love God wants you to have for your spouse.

It involves being 'united' with one's partner – the Hebrew word means literally 'glued' together – not just physically and biologically but emotionally, psychologically, socially and spiritually. This is the Christian context of the 'one-flesh' union.

Most importantly, the Bible says, "And husbands should love their wives like that. They should love their wives as they love their own bodies. The man who loves his wife loves himself, because no one ever hates his own body, but feeds and takes care of it. And that is what Christ does for the church because we are parts of his body.

The Scriptures say, That is why a man will leave his father and mother and join his wife, and the two people will become one." That secret truth is very important—I am talking about Christ and the church. But each one of you must love his wife as he loves himself. And a wife must respect her husband". (Ephesians 5:28)

The biblical doctrine of marriage is the most exciting and positive one that exists. It is also the most romantic view. It sets before us God's perfect plan. "Jesus answered, "Surely you have read this in the Scriptures: When God made the world, 'he made people male and female.' And God said, 'That is why a man will leave his father and mother and be joined to his wife. And the two people will become one." (Matthew 19:4)

LET THE LOVE OF GOD
BE YOUR GUIDE

The Bible says, *"I may speak in different languages, whether human or even of angels. But if I don't have love, I am only a noisy bell or a ringing cymbal. I may have the gift of prophecy, I may understand all secrets and know everything there is to know, and I may have faith so great that I can move mountains. But even with all this, if I don't have love, I am nothing. I may give away everything I have to help others, and I may even give my body as an offering to be burned. But I gain nothing by doing all this if I don't have love.*

Love is patient and kind. Love is not jealous, it does not brag, and it is not proud. Love is not rude, it is not selfish, and it cannot be made angry easily. Love does not remember wrongs done against it. Love is never happy when others do wrong, but it is always happy with the truth. Love never gives up on people. It never stops trusting, never loses hope, and never quits.

Love will never end. But all those gifts will come to an end—even the gift of prophecy, the gift of speaking in different kinds of languages, and the gift of knowledge. These will all end because this knowledge and these prophecies we have are not complete. But when perfection comes, the things that are not complete will end.

When I was a child, I talked like a child, I thought like a child, and I made plans like a child. When I became a man, I stopped those childish ways. It is the same with us. Now we see God as if we are looking at a reflection in a mirror. But then, in the future, we will see him right before our eyes. Now I know only a part, but at that time I will know fully, as God has known me. So these three things continue: faith, hope, and love. And the greatest of these is love. (1 Corinthians 13:1-13) ERV.

The Shulammite woman use an allegory to describe true love, *"Set me like a seal upon your heart, like a seal upon your arm; for love is as strong as death, jealousy is as hard and cruel as Sheol (the place of the dead). Its flashes are flashes of fire, a most vehement flame [the very flame of the Lord]! Many waters cannot quench love, neither can floods drown it. If a man would offer all the goods of his house for love, he would be utterly scorned and despised." (Song of Solomon 8:6-7). AMPC.*

Love is as STRONG as death. Only death can break the power of love. Many waters can not quench love. No matter how deep or turbulent the waters of tribulation and affliction are, they can not drown love. *"When you have troubles, I am with you. When you cross rivers, you will not be hurt. When you walk through fire, you will not be burned; the flames will not hurt you". (Isaiah 43:2). ERV.* Neither can the floods of crisis drown love...... No disaster or satanic storm can destroy true love.

Love can not be bought. Love is unconditional and it is priceless, it is a gift from God. The love of God was shed into our heart by the Holy Spirit. *"And this hope will never disappoint us. We know this because God has poured out his love to fill our hearts through the Holy Spirit he gave us". (Romans 5:5). ERV.*

I believe that love is the greatest weapon we have against hatred and anti-marriage forces. May I ask you a question? If a husband and a wife fight or have a misunderstanding, who should apologize?

Answer: The person who was wrong. If you believe that answer, then you have just failed the entrance examination into the institution of marriage. The correct answer is this: The person who loves the most will apologize first. *"Hatred causes arguments, but love overlooks all wrongs". (Proverbs 10:12). ERV.*

People of God, remember the Bible says that, *"Love is patient and kind. Love is not jealous, it does not brag, and it is not proud. Love is not rude, it is not selfish, and it cannot be made angry easily. Love does not remember wrongs done against it. Love is never happy when others do wrong, but it is always happy with the truth. Love never gives up on people. It never stops trusting, never loses hope, and never quits". (1 Corinthians 13:4)*

Let me challenge you today that if you truly and honestly love your spouse, you will be determined to make your marriage work and no anti-marriage force can come between you to cut anything asunder.

What is Agape Love and Why it Changes Everything.

"So we know the love that God has for us, and we trust that love. God is love. Everyone who lives in love lives in God, and God lives in them". (1 John 4:16). ERV.

Agape love is selfless love, the love God wants to have isn't just an emotion but conscious act of the will....... a deliberate decision on our part to put others ahead of ourselves. This is the kind of love God has for us and wants you to have for your spouse.

I'm beginning to think that love is not what the world think it means. Okay, now that I've written that out loud I realize it doesn't make sense out of context, so let me go back a little bit.

I've been having trouble sleeping lately (big surprise). When that happens, I usually pass the night trying to pray through questions I have about faith and life, and lately I've been praying about love. You see, I have known great love, intimately, purposely, lavished on me with unwavering determination for the past 29 years of marital life from my wife, Oladunni.

I've thought about it a lot, and read about love and the meanings of love. I've also studied the Greek terms for love, especially the Greek word agape which is supposed to be the highest expression of love, a pure, selfless, unconditional thing. But as I meditate on the love I've experienced, examining how it shaped and reshaped me, even agape seems not enough to explain it.

May I encourage you to pray to God to give you true love for your spouse. Ask the Lord to teach you how to love your spouse and meet his/her needs (emotional, financial, material, physical and spiritual. I know that the love you have for your spouse will cause you to continually for him/her in prayer. As you do this from a heart of love, God will give you the victory.

The Bible says, *"Two people are better than one. When two people work together, they get more work done. If one person falls, the other person can reach out to help. But those who are alone when they fall have no one to help them. If two people sleep together, they will be warm. But a person sleeping alone will not be warm. An enemy might be able to defeat one person, but two people can stand back-to-back to defend each other. And three people are even stronger. They are like a rope that has three parts wrapped together—it is very hard to break".* *(Ecclesiastes 4:9)*

The Truth About Marriage

You or anyone you marry has a weakness. Only God does not have a weakness. So if you focus on your spouse's weakness you can't get the best out of his strength.

Everyone has a dark history. No one is an angel. When you get married or you want to get married stop digging into someone's past. What matters most is the present life of your partner. Old things have passed away. Forgive and forget. Focus on the present and the future.

Every marriage has its own challenges. Marriage is not a bed of roses. Every good marriage has gone through its own test of blazing fire. True love proves in times of challenges. Fight for your marriage. Make up your mind to stay with your spouse in times of need. Remember the vow *For better for worse*. In sickness and in health be there.

Every marriage has different levels of success. Don't compare your marriage with any one else. We can never be equal. Some will be far, some behind. To avoid marriage stresses, be patient, work hard and with time your marriage dreams shall come true.

To get married is declaring war and you must declare war against enemies of marriage. Some enemies of marriage are:

Ignorance
Prayerlessness
Unforgiveness
Third party influence
Stinginess
Stubbornness
Lack of love
Rudeness
Laziness
Disrespect
Cheating

Be ready to fight to maintain your marriage zone.

There is no perfect marriage. There is no ready made marriage. Marriage is hard work. Volunteer yourself to work daily on it. Marriage is like a car that needs proper maintenance and proper service. If this is not done it will break down somewhere exposing the owner to danger or some unhealthy circumstances. Let us not be careless about our marriages.

God cannot give you a complete person you desire. He gives you the person in the form of raw materials in order for you to mould the person that you desire. This can only be achieved through prayer, love and Patience.

Getting married is taking a huge risk. You can not predict what will happen in the future. Situations may change so leave room for adjustments. Husband can lose his good job or you may fail to have babies. All these require you to be prayerful otherwise you might divorce.

Marriage is not a contract. It is permanent. It needs total commitment. Love is the glue that sticks the couple together. Divorce start in the mind and the devil feeds the mind. Never ever entertain thoughts of getting a divorce. Never threaten your spouse with divorce. Choose to remain married. God hates divorce.

Every marriage has a price to pay. Marriage is like a bank account. It is the money that you deposit that you withdraw. If you don't deposit love, peace and care into your marriage, you are not a candidate for a blissful home.

So today, may I encourage you to pray for your marriages and ask God to help you and your spouse where you are lacking in any of the above listed secrets of a good home in Jesus name. Amen.

The Bible says, *"Jesus answered, "Have you not read that he who created them from the beginning made them Male and Female, and said, 'Therefore a man shall leave his father and his mother and host fast to his wife, and the two shall become one flesh. What therefore God has joined together, let not man separate." (Matthew 19: 4-6).*

Reasons Why Your Wedding Rings Matter More than You Think.

As a family and marriage counsellor that is passionate in marriage, homes, children and as minister of the Lord Jesus Christ , I have witnessed many wedding ceremonies. It's one of my favourite passion to see a man and a woman emerging into reality of becoming husband and wife. I'm always eager to seat in the front row seat to witness one of the most beautiful milestone a new couple will ever experience as husband and wife.

I love watching the groom trying to choke back tears when he gets the first glimpse of his bride walking down the aisle. I love how the couple barely hears a word the officiating minister is saying during the whole ceremony because they're blissfully lost in each other's eyes and in the magnitude of the moment. I love everything a wedding represents.

One of the most profound parts of the ceremony happens when the Best Man and the Maid of Honour hand the wedding rings to the officiant. The officiating minister place the rings on top of the Bible and talk about how beautiful they are and will usually crack a joke by saying something like, "*He went to Diamond Heaven*" (which only makes sense if you have Diamond Heavens commercials in your area).

The officiating minister then go on to talk about all at the rings represent and I watch as the couple nervously place the rings on each other's hands and stare at them with a look that says, "*I'm NEVER taking this off!*"

It saddens me that so many couples do take them off.

Sometimes it happens because of very practical reasons like skin conditions or work environments that aren't conducive to jewellery, but most of the time, a person simply prefers not to wear it and invents justifications for why it's not really important. Just like Frodo and the Hobbits learned in Tolkien's epic "*Lord of the Rings*" series, sometimes **a ring can have a lot more significance than you see on the surface!**

As we are advocates for stronger marriage, **my wife Oladunni** and I always encouraging couples to do everything in their power to protect and strengthen their marriage, and YES, this includes wearing wedding rings. **We believe wearing a wedding ring is more important than you might think for the following reasons** (in no particular order).

1. **Whether or not you're wearing a ring is one of the FIRST things people notice when they meet you and they'll often make assumptions about your availability and your commitment to your marriage based on the ring's presence or absence.**

    I know about a grandmother that has been a widow for decades, but early in her marriage, the husband cheated on her by having multiple affairs. She's never fully healed from those wounds.

    To this day, when she is talking about a man whether he's a person she knows or a celebrity in the public eye (even pastors), one of her first observations is always either "*He's always wearing his wedding ring.*" Or "*He doesn't wear a wedding ring.*" She makes assumptions about the man's integrity and commitment to his wife based on the ring's presence or absence.

    While she might be an extreme example, many people will make similar assumptions. We should live to cater to other people's assumptions, but **if the simple act of wearing a ring could prevent misconceptions, then why wouldn't you wear it?**

2. **I believe that your wedding ring *reveals how a wedding ring can impact your marriage on a daily basis. Your wedding ring is a daily reminder to you that every decision you make will impact your spouse in some way.***

    A ring is a tangible symbol of the permanent place your spouse should hold in your heart, your schedule and every part of your life. From the moment you said, "I do," every aspect of your life is now connected to your spouse.

You're "One" according to the Bible. Everything you do with your time, your words, your money, etc. will impact him/her in some way so the ring is a simple reminder that everything you touch will touch your marriage.

3. **Your ring is a symbol of RESPECT for your spouse.**

Respect in marriage isn't measured only by what we say. It's often the silent acts and actions that speak the loudest. Respect in marriage is communicated constantly (since marriage is a constant relationship).

The ring is one simple way to communicate that respect **ESPECIALLY** when your spouse has asked you to wear it and/or communicated that it's important to them. If your spouse has asked you to wear it, and you consistently deny their request, then you are consistently communicating disrespect and disregard for his/her feelings.

4. **Your ring is a first line of defence against infidelity.**

A wedding ring isn't a fail-proof safeguard against infidelity, and it's certainly a simple first line of defence. Wearing a ring subtly communicates the message that, ***"I'm married. I'm committed. My marriage matters to me."***

If you're trying to be "married undercover" by keeping your marital status a mystery in public, that's NOT healthy. Some people (who have no respect for marriage) may still proposition you while you're wearing a ring, but you can prevent many unnecessary temptations by simply wearing it.

5. **Your ring is a visible symbol to your kids that your marriage matters.**

If you have children, one of the most important lessons you can teach them is what a marriage should look like. Have the kind of marriage that makes them want to get married someday! *Show your kids the beauty of a husband and wife committed to each other in both public and private.*

This requires MUCH more than just a ring, but the ring will be something they notice and it can provide opportunities for you to talk about why you wear it and what it represents.

6. **There aren't really any good reasons for NOT wearing it!**

Like I said at the beginning, there are some practical exceptions to this rule, but overall, when it's simply a matter of preference, why not wear your ring? There are so many positive ways it can help your marriage and really no downside.

If your attitude isn't "*Well, I shouldn't have to,*" and instead you think, "*I want to always do everything in my power to respect my husband/wife and protect my marriage,*" then you'll be on the right track.

Marriage Decisions to Make Today

Did you know that most divorces are the result of what researchers call "non-severe circumstances"? That means the marriage-ending circumstances are not related to severe problems like abuse, abandonment or adultery. Instead, they are because of fights about money, kids, sex and other emotional issues. These are emotional decisions. They happen in the heat of the moment.

One of the most important characteristics of a healthy marriage is to make decisions without regard to emotions. Emotions are fickle and unpredictable. They may be very real, but they can also be very wrong.

But at the same time, we're humans. We are emotional creatures. So, how can you keep emotions from impacting the health of your marriage? The best approach is to pre-make your decisions now. Instead of making decisions based on how you feel, make them based on what is right and what is best for your relationship.

Here are some decisions to make today about your marriage:

1. We will never threaten divorce. You were married for life, so take divorce off the table. Don't use threats of divorce as leverage to get your spouse to do something. In fact, take the word out of your vocabulary altogether. Work out your problems without using that word.

2. We will never go to bed angry. Work out your disagreements on a daily basis or resentment will begin to fester. If you can't find a solution, submit to Godly counsel. There will always be times in a marriage where you can't work out problems on your own, so get help. Getting help is not a sign of weakness but of wisdom.

3. We will never "agree to disagree." Marriage is the longest journey you'll take in your life, but if one spouse is going one direction and the other spouse goes the other way, you will always have conflict. Seek agreement by seeking the

Lord together. Submit to God and godly counsel until the two of you can get on the same page.

4. We will respect and celebrate our differences. You are two distinct individuals, which means you won't always look at the world the same way. Do not dishonour each other or disrespect each other because your spouse thinks differently than you. Refuse to judge each other or talk bad about each other. Instead, be thankful for the ways you are different. It makes you a better team.

5. We will give each other the right to complain and be honest without paying a price. Think of yourself as a customer relations counter for your marriage. If your customer—your spouse—brings a complaint to you, then listen to that complaint and work to make it right. Accept it with a good attitude. Don't roll your eyes. Don't be defensive. Don't shame your spouse for being honest with you.

6. We will be faithful to each other. Faithfulness means more than just sexual faithfulness (though of course that is a big part of your marriage vows). Faithfulness also refers to your emotions. Even during times of frustration or difficulty, never let your heart be turned away from each other to another person.

7. We will develop healthy relationships with fellow believers. If you want to know what your marriage will look like in five years, observe the couples you're spending time with today. Divorces run in packs. You want friends who will encourage you to do the right thing, even during hard times. You also need to remain connected to a Bible-believing local church where you can hear God's Word preached on a weekly basis. Church is where you'll find your best friends.

8. We will make our decisions together. The two of you are equal partners. There should not be one spouse who is dominant and one spouse who is more submissive. When you are making any significant decision, both of you have

equal input and both of you respect each other's opinions. Never bully each other to change or influence a decision.

9. We will prioritize our marriage above everything else. Apart from your relationship with God, your marriage is the most important relationship in your life. It is more important than your children, your job, your personal interests or your hobbies. Determine to work hard to meet each other's needs, and refuse to sacrifice your marriage for anything or anyone else.

10. We will base our marriage on Christ-like love. His love never fails. Marriage is a covenant designed by God. It is sacrificial and permanent. It is not a relationship of convenience. The vows "for better or for worse, for richer or for poorer, in sickness and in health" are covenant vows. That means your marriage is based on the decision to love and cherish each other and not on feelings, convenience or comfort.

Don't make important decisions in your marriage based on emotions. If you do, you'll regret it. Make these ten important decisions now and you'll create a marriage strong enough to withstand difficulties, disagreements and fleeting emotions.

Chapter 1
Marriage Institution

Marriage institution is the only institution that you receive your certificate before the course begins. It is the institution that will test your faith, behaviour, attitude, endurance, patience, belief system etc.

We made covenant with one another and we have to be committed to it by God's grace, with understanding and wisdom. According to the books of (Proverb 31, Proverb 14:1, 1 Corinthians 11:3, Ephesian 5:23-24, Titus 2:2-8) these are the original role of a married woman and the man.

The divine principles and the older ones should be an inspiration to younger generations more so, it is our test of faith. Marriage is the only institution that God ordained and it is a blessings and favour. Marriage is our training ground.

The man is the head, Priest, King and a Leader. Woman cannot contest or compete with them. Men are not perfect and women are not perfect either. We have gone through a lots together and we are still standing, it is about the Will of God not our own will or emotion. How we feel or how it should be or what people said or our thought however, no condition is permanent, we are all learning and growing everyday.

We just need to learn how to appreciate our differences, strengths and weaknesses and give ourselves time, space and focus. Divorce and living single or separating from one another is not the best solution. A virtuous woman built her home with God's wisdom. The fear of God is the beginning of wisdom.

It is about relationship with God and obeying His laws/commandments that matters. Love one another, It is about patience, understanding and endurance, it is about tolerance and not with provocation, arrogance, pride, competition, violence, pretence, deceit nor suffering silent but by prayers and seeking for help when needed.

We all need one another as the Lord stated that it is not good to leave man alone.....the male is for strength while the female is for comfort. May the Lord answer all your prayers. May his grace and wisdom keep us together in Jesus name

Secrets of a Successful Marriage

1. **Dream a Dream.** If you want your marriage to grow and to be its best, husband and wife need to create a vision for it and your life together.

2. **Get Tough.** Marriage takes a lot of work, and a couple must be willing to fully commit to making the marriage strong.

3. **Maximize the Trust Factor.** Learn how to be truthful and trustworthy for your husband or wife, and how to trust one another in return.

4. **Get Healthy.** Marriages have a much greater chance of being successful if both people are emotionally healthy. If

one or both of you have personal issues or an unhealthy self-concept, consider seeing a counsellor.

5. **Work on Chemistry.** Keep the romance strong in your marriage. Discover the reasons you fell in love with each other and build on those.

6. **Learn to Talk.** Communication is invaluable in a strong marriage. Take the time to learn good communication skills and use them in your relationship.

7. **Work it Through.** Even in the best marriages, conflict will happen. The key to getting through the tough times is to learn the skills of conflict resolution and to come up with a strategy in your marriage.

8. **Negotiate a Mutually Satisfying Sexual Relationship.** Both you and your husband need to be willing to work on this aspect of your relationship. May I   recommend including buying a book on marital sex, seeking counselling if needed and improving communication.

9. **Get Connected.** Although children can be a drain on a marriage relationship, they can also be the source of joy if their role is viewed correctly.

10. **Pursue Spirituality.** Spiritual intimacy in marriage is another great step toward marital fulfilment.

Marriage Secrets of Successful Couples

1. **Successful couples are positive about each other.** I believe they don't speak negatively of their spouse to anyone, and they encourage one another rather than criticize.

2. **Successful couples apologize as soon as possible and bounce back from disagreements quickly.** One of my friends told me that his mentor taught him early on in marriage that the stronger person apologizes first, even if

they are only 1% wrong. This secret helps disarm the conflict almost immediately.

3. **They grow and try new things together.** It's easy to grow apart if you're not growing together. Learning something new together will often bring new joys and new ways of connecting. Now that our three boys are grown, and left home. My wife, Oladunni and I have begun traveling and exploring new horizons together.

4. **Each person in a successful relationship takes care of themselves.** They are proactive in dealing with their own emotional baggage, past hurt and anything that would limit them from being a healthy person. They don't let their stuff get in the way.

5. **Successful couples try to see things from each other's point of view.** They don't become defensive, but they practice empathy. When my wife and I don't understand the other's point of view, we've leant to spend time together and gently discussing the situations and our respective feelings in order to come to a place of empathy. We actively show one another we care by trying to see things from the other's point of view.

6. **They commit to forever.** They never threaten to leave because they don't consider leaving an option. Opening the door to divorce mentally has an immediate negative impact on a marriage. It weakens your resolve to stay. Love is an act of the will, and resolve is essential.

7. **They make each other a priority and don't take each other for granted.** They put in effort, and they never stop dating. This takes intentionality and effort, but it is effort that produces great results in the relationship. I believe that couples that do this will never be lonely in their marriage.

Chapter 2
Principles Of Successful Couples.

Happiness is not the most important thing. Everyone wants to be happy, but happiness will come and go. Successful couples learn to intentionally do things that will bring happiness back when life pulls it away.

Couples discover the value in just showing up. When things get tough and couples don't know what to do, they need to hang in there and be there for their spouse. Time has a way of helping couples work things out by providing opportunities to reduce stress and overcome challenges.

If you do what you always do, you will get same result. Wise couples have learned that you have to approach problems differently to get different results. Often, minor changes in approach, attitude and actions make the biggest difference in marriage.

Your attitude does matter. Changing behaviour is important, but so is changing attitudes. Bad attitudes often drive bad feelings and actions.

Change your mind, change your marriage. How couples think and what they believe about their spouse affects how they perceive the other. What they expect and how they treat their spouse matters greatly.

The grass is greenest where you water it. Successful couples have learned to resist the grass is greener myth — i.e., someone else will make me happy. They have learned to put their energy into making themselves and their marriage better.

You can change your marriage by changing yourself. Veteran couples have learned that trying to change their spouse is like trying to push a rope — almost impossible. Often, the only person we can change in our marriage is ourselves.

Love is a verb, not just a feeling. Everyday life wears away the "feel good side of marriage." Feelings, like happiness, will fluctuate. But, real love is based on a couple's vows of commitment: "For better or for worse" — when it feels good and when it doesn't.

Marriage is often about fighting the battle between your ears. Successful couples have learned to resist holding grudges and bringing up the past. They remember that they married an imperfect person — and so did their spouse.

A crisis doesn't mean the marriage is over. Crises are like storms: loud, scary and dangerous. But to get through a storm you have to keep driving. A crisis can be a new beginning. It's out of pain that great people and marriages are produced.

The Rituals to make you Happy Couple and Stay Spicy.

I believe we all need to understand that relationships are always changing and growing as each person grow and shift into their purpose. Staying connected with marital rituals is worth investing in, to maintain healthy relationships. Without this rituals, it is easy to feel distant or separate from your spouse.

May I share few marital rituals with you that will enhance and make your marriage sweet and spicy. For instance, each evening, list three good things that your spouse has done that day to make your life sweeter. I know that by doing this daily, you will build up positive regard towards each other and assuredly it will be less likely to fight over small issues.

Every couple that is fond of their spouse tend to overlook small issues and don't use resentment over them. This rituals will help both husband and wife to remember the good things in their relationship on a day to day basis. There is a way that husband and wife need to speak to one another in an effective manner to subtly and non-verbally communication for your desire for relationship change can involve softening.

Softening vastly do with your tone of voice, language, behaviour and even your body posture. Being intentional to soften will send a message to your partner that you are trying and the impact can sometimes be dramatic. Soft is comfortable to embrace. Soft is easier to understand. Soft is safe and enjoyable to be near.

This is what the Scriptures say, *"When you talk, don't say anything bad. But say the good things that people need, whatever will help them grow stronger. Then what you say will be a blessing to those who hear you. And don't make the Holy Spirit sad. God gave you his Spirit as proof that you belong to him and that he will keep you safe until the day he makes you free. Never be bitter, angry, or mad.*

Never shout angrily or say things to hurt others. Never do anything evil. Be kind and loving to each other. Forgive each other the same as God forgave you through Christ." (Ephesians 4:29-32). ERV

There Are Things you are not suppose to do in Marital Relationship.

I thank God that by His grace, I have been married to my wife for the past 29 years and now realised that there are actions husband and wife should do in order to maintain the joy and peace in their relationship. Also equally important, there are things that couple actually don't have to do, that they may have assumed were necessary for their marriage.

When my wife and I just got married 29 years ago, just like any new married couple. We thought that we have to be each others everything. We feels as though our life stops in other for this new life to begins as a newly married couple. May I tell you the honest truth, both thoughts are incorrect.

The fact is that newly wed couples sometimes bring unrealistic ideas as well as expectation into the Sacred partnership and then were confused as to why their relationship is not up to standard as expected because of certain behaviours or habit you are not suppose to continue after you get married.

My point is that you need to be aware of your own personal limitation and understand that you don't have supernatural power. You can not save, heal or change another person, it is only God that can do all that by His Spirit through you.

However, you can love, support and share your life with your spouse. May I share with you, my experience, knowledge and understanding of marital relationship for you to create a happy, long lasting healthy union and good family. Remember, as a married man or woman, there are things you are not suppose to do in marriage which I will discus with you further in this book that will help and encourage you on your marital journey especially newly married, those that have married for quite a while or those that want to get marry soon.

Hear this, partnership in marriage means both individual are bringing something into the relationship. The truth is that you should not enter into marriage for what you can get but what you can give. Many people get into marital relationship for what they can get but at the end of it all, it created disappointment, bitterness and divorce.

May I say this to those that are yet to tie the knot, that you should have your own sense of peace and happiness before you say " I DO ". Marriage is an eye opener.

Chapter 3
Why Wives Must Read The Context Of (Ephesians 5:22) With Understanding.

"Wives, submit to your own husbands as you do to the Lord" (Ephesians 5:22) For many, it's a troubling or ludicrous command. Cynics quote this verse to prove that the Bible is archaic and irrelevant.

A biblically illiterate husband will quotes this verse to keep his wife in a subservient role, insisting her opinion has no value and her contribution to the household is limited to cooking, cleaning, and keeping herself available to his sexual whims. Christian women with husbands who are not church attenders struggle with how to respond to the idea of submission.

Instead of skipping over it, let's put (Ephesians 5:22), in context. Upon further examination, I believe you'll discover this verse and its surrounding passages are all about empowerment for every member of the family.

Let's begin with the nine words immediately preceding that verse. (Ephesians 5:21), says quite plainly, "Submit to one another out of reverence for Christ." The apostle Paul was writing to believers in the church at Ephesus and all believers everywhere. He expected us to have the heart of a servant and put first the needs of others.

Then after introducing the concept of submitting to one another, Paul turns his attention to the family, which is the building block of a healthy society. He gives three examples of how submission works in real life for wives, husbands, and kids. Read them for yourself:

"Wives, submit to your own husbands as you do to the Lord. For the husband is the head of the wife as Christ is the head of the church, his body, of which he is the Saviour" (Ephesians 5:22-23).

"Husbands, love your wives, just as Christ loved the church and gave himself up for her...In this same way, husbands ought to love their wives as their own bodies. He who loves his wife loves himself" (Ephesians 5:25, 28).

"Children, obey your parents in the Lord, for this is right" (Ephesians 6:1).

Men, women, and children have different needs, so Paul explains how to honour and affirm each of them differently. Children need instruction. Women need to feel cherished. Men need to lead.

Submission is all about putting the needs of other members of your family ahead of your own. But today's culture doesn't place a very high value on others. Selfishness, misplaced priorities, and exhaustion keep us from nurturing our own submissive hearts and we have nothing left to give to the people we love most.

- Busy parents sometimes don't have the time or energy to instruct and discipline their kids, but that's what they need. Our kids are counting on us to teach them right from wrong.

- Distracted husbands sometimes forget to do the little things (and the big things) to express love to our wives. But a husband's sacrificial love for his bride is critical for a healthy marriage.

- Exhausted wives sometimes make family decisions without any input from their husbands. She's trying to manage a household and can't even get his attention. He feels out of the loop and the family loses his leadership. And he loses their respect.

Can you see the immediate benefits of Ephesians chapter 5 to both a wife and husband? Some theologians call it "mutual submission." Others don't like that term, but it's a pretty accurate paraphrase of how the Bible describes a successful marriage.

The truth is that the husband feels respected and the wife feels loved. Both are looking for the best in each other and looking out for each other.

Pray over Your Marriage

The Scripture says, *"Two are better than one, because they have a good return for their labour. If either of them falls down, one can help the other up. But pity anyone who falls and has no one to help them up. Also, if two lie down together, they will keep warm. But how can one keep warm alone? Though one may be overpowered, two can defend themselves. A cord of three strands is not quickly broken." (Ecclesiastes 4: 9-12).*

The Bible tells us that two are better than one. We know God's Word to be true, but if we are human and honest, we will often admit that marriage is hard. It doesn't always seem like two really are better than one, does it?

Your wife wants you to understand that although she may be strong, assertive, secure, and spiritually growing, she still needs you to actively lead her to the cross. It's a no-brainer that men and women process and express themselves differently when it comes to spiritual matters, but your wife needs you to step up to the plate and serve as her spiritual warrior!

She needs you to pray over her, for you to be growing in your knowledge of the Word so that you can be a truth-speaker in her life, and she needs you to encourage her to seek after God with all her heart. Making our marriage stronger takes intentionality and I believe in prayer. When we are intentionally humbling ourselves and praying for our spouse, our heart grows more soft and pliable. God is able to work in my heart as well as in my spouse.

But should we pray? What if marriage is so hard we can hardly utter words of hope? This is where praying God's Word comes into play. Learning to pray God's Word has been something God has used in my life when I was desperate and without words.

Praying God's Word gives me the words when I have none, but also gives me the confidence to pray because I know I am praying in alignment with His Will if I'm praying from His Word.

I believe that Praying God's Word is for the weak and broken like me, Charles. Praying God's Word is for me and you as we are the children of the Most High!

And even if your marriage is strong and you don't need help finding words to pray, the Bible verses listed on the next page can help you with new ideas of how to pray for your marriage.

Prayer for Your Marriage!

"Have I not commanded you? Be strong and courageous. Do not be afraid; do not be discouraged, for the Lord your God will be with you wherever you go." (Joshua 1:9). (Lord, make us strong for you in Jesus name). Amen.

"By wisdom a house is built, and through understanding it is established; through knowledge its rooms are filled with rare and beautiful treasures." (Proverbs 24:3-4). (Lord, may our home be built on your wisdom in Jesus name). Amen.

"Blessed is the one who does not walk in step with the wicked or stand in the way that sinners take or sit in the company of mockers, but whose delight is in the law of the Lord, and who meditates on his law day and night. That person is like a tree planted by streams of water, which yields its fruit in season and whose leaf does not wither—whatever they do prospers." (Psalm 1:1-3).

(Lord, may our delight be in you, may we meditate on your law day and night. When we do so, our marriage and our family will be like a tree planted by streams of water, which yields fruit in its season and whose leaf does not wither in Jesus name.) Amen.

"Create in me a pure heart, O God, and renew a steadfast spirit within me." (Psalm 51:10). (Lord, create in both of us a pure heart, seeking you first in all things in Jesus name.) Amen.

"How delightful is your love, my sister, my bride! How much more pleasing is your love than wine, and the fragrance of your perfume more than any spice!" (Song of Solomon 4:10). (May we delight in our love for one another everyday in Jesus name.) Amen.

"As a young man marries a young woman, so will your Builder marry you; as a bridegroom rejoices over his bride, so will your God rejoice over you." (Isaiah 62:5). (May we rejoice over one another and in turn, rest in the knowledge that you, God, rejoice over us as your children in Jesus name.) Amen.

"Love is patient, love is kind. It does not envy, it does not boast, it is not proud. It does not dishonour others, it is not self-seeking, it is not easily angered, it keeps no record of wrongs. Love does not delight in evil but rejoices with the truth. It always protects, always trusts, always hopes, always perseveres. Love never fails." (1 Corinthians 14:4-8).

(Lord, give us your kind of love for our spouse and for our families. Grow us in patience, kindness, honour, service, and may we never keep a record of wrongs. May our love never fail because it is your love in us in Jesus name.) Amen.

"Submit to one another out of reverence for Christ. Wives, submit yourselves to your own husbands as you do to the Lord. For the husband is the head of the wife as Christ is the head of the church, his body, of which he is the Saviour. Now as the church submits to Christ, so also wives should submit to their husbands in everything.

Husbands, love your wives, just as Christ loved the church and gave himself up for her to make her holy, cleansing her by the washing with water through the word, and to present her to himself as a radiant church, without stain or wrinkle or any other blemish, but holy and blameless. In this same way, husbands ought to love their wives as their own bodies. He who loves his wife loves himself. After all, no one ever hated their own body, but they feed and care for their body, just as Christ does the church— for we are members of his body.

'For this reason a man will leave his father and mother and be united to his wife, and the two will become one flesh.' This is a profound mystery—but I am talking about Christ and the church. However, each one of you also must love his wife as he loves himself, and the wife must respect her husband." (Ephesians 5:21-33). (Lord, may we joyfully submit to one another out of reverence for Christ. May we love like Jesus in Jesus name.) Amen.

"Do nothing out of selfish ambition or vain conceit. Rather, in humility value others above yourselves, not looking to your own interests but each of you to the interests of the others. In your relationships with one another, have the same mind set as Christ Jesus: Who, being in very nature God, did not consider equality with God something to be used to his own advantage; rather, he made himself nothing by taking the very nature of a servant, being made in human likeness." (Philippians 2:3-7).

(Lord, help us to not do anything out of selfish ambition. Give us humble hearts toward one another, not looking to our own interests, but to the interests of our spouse. Give us the mind of Christ in Jesus name). Amen.

"For he has rescued us from the dominion of darkness and brought us into the kingdom of the Son he loves, in whom we have redemption, the forgiveness of sins." (Colossians 1:13-14). (Lord, may we never forget that you rescued us from the dominion of darkness. May we show that same forgiveness to our spouse in Jesus name). Amen

Chapter 4
The Truth Concerning Marriage.

Marriage get better or worse, they don't stand still. May I ask you! What are you actively doing to make your marriage better? If the honest answer is nothing, then it may be heading in the wrong direction.

In marriage, doing what seems easy in the moment often isn't what's best for long term. There is a delicate nature to marriage as I can understand because I've married for the past 29 years. The truth is, there's a delicate nature to all relationships.

It is so easy to forget that and take one another for granted, then stop being careful, stop being mindful, stop being protective. Stop and embrace the unrushed yes of investing in those we love. The Scriptures wisely remind us that "all our busy rushing ends in nothing" (Psalm 39:6).

It is very true that the unravelling can happen so quickly when we refuse to push the pause button. For every relationship to stand the test of time, you must be having what I call Conversational threads time to time.

May I encourage you to understand that Conversational threads are what make up the fabric of relationship. Every husband and wife must take time out, make time-to talk so that both husband and wife can be fulfilled in their marital relationship.

One of the reasons I wrote this book is to help husband and wife know and understand ways to quickly improve their marriage. whether your marriage is in the pits, good, great or awesome, there are ways you can step up to the next level.

Let me be real with you, reading alone of what to do will not do you any good but the application that stems from a place of love, that is, love for yourself and for your spouse. Every husband and wife that want their marriage to stand the test of time need to honour one another differences.

Yes, I said it, honour your differences because no two people are alike. We are unique individuals and that is to be celebrated and honoured. The fact that your spouse is different from you should be a joy.

The truth I want you to understand is that the two of you compliment one another. You are unique and genuine individuals but together, you are a fantastic unit. Your differences is easier to handle when they are honoured. It is difficult when you are looking to your spouse to conform and be like you.

May I encourage you that Marriage is beautiful when you abide by the rule of the One who ordain marital relationship. But nowadays, there are statements from people not ready for marriage.

Let me ask you this! Have you ever been in a conversation with someone and what they argue about makes you cringe? Those are awkward; right? I can tell you now that the issue of marriage is one of those topics that produces cringe-worthy answers.

Often, many people use books or movies to give them a framework for marriage but that is not all it takes to have a good marital relationship. The truth is, until you follow the guidelines of the God who institute marriage, your marriage may not be the best that you want it to be. Let me share with you some of the reasons both husband and wife need one another!

I believe that marriage is one of the most rewarding joint institution that you can experience and again it may also be very challenging at times. The reality of good marital relationship is that your spouse is the first point of contact to discuss any issue that may be affecting your relationship.

That is why the scriptures say, "Be willing to serve each other out of respect for Christ. Wives, be willing to serve your husbands the same as the Lord. A husband is the head of his wife, just as Christ is the head of the church. Christ is the Saviour of the church, which is his body. The church serves under Christ, so it is the same with you wives.

You should be willing to serve your husbands in everything. Husbands, love your wives the same as Christ loved the church and gave his life for it. He died to make the church holy. He used the telling of the Good News to make the church clean by washing it with water.

Christ died so that he could give the church to himself like a bride in all her beauty. He died so that the church could be holy and without fault, with no evil or sin or any other thing wrong in it.

And husbands should love their wives like that. They should love their wives as they love their own bodies. The man who loves his wife loves himself, because no one ever hates his own body, but feeds and takes care of it. And that is what Christ does for the church because we are parts of his body.

The Scriptures say, *"That is why a man will leave his father and mother and join his wife, and the two people will become one." That secret truth is very important. I am talking about Christ and the church. But each one of you must love his wife as he loves himself. And a wife must respect her husband." (Ephesians 5:21-33).*

Let me be real with you and go there, know what I mean? You know that at times your spouse is not on the same page with you. Sometimes you are at logger heads that you can not hear each other. May I encourage you that during those period that you are feeling alone, unheard and thinking of giving up on your marriage!

Remember God hate DIVORCE. There is no compromise with such situation. You need to go to God to sort you out. He is the originator of marriage and I believe He will teach you what to do.

The Truths About Good Marriage you Should Know.

I can say with humility in my heart and with the grace of God, that I have under my belt over 29 years of good hard work marital relationship with my wife, and blessed with 3 Godly sons. (Yes, to the same God fearing, fantastic woman of God. The day I understood the Scriptures that say, "Be willing to serve each other out of respect for Christ. Wives, be willing to serve your husbands the same as the Lord. A husband is the head of his wife, just as Christ is the head of the church.

Christ is the Saviour of the church, which is his body. The church serves under Christ, so it is the same with you wives. You should be willing to serve your husbands in everything. Husbands, love your wives the same as Christ loved the church and gave his life for it. He died to make the church holy. He used the telling of the Good News to make the church clean by washing it with water. Christ died so that he could give the church to himself like a bride in all her beauty. He died so that the church could be holy and without fault, with no evil or sin or any other thing wrong in it.

And husbands should love their wives like that. They should love their wives as they love their own bodies. The man who loves his wife loves himself, because no one ever hates his own body, but feeds and takes care of it. And that is what Christ does for the church because we are parts of his body. The Scriptures say, "That is why a man will leave his father and mother and join his wife, and the two people will become one." That secret truth is very important—I am talking about Christ and the church. But each one of you must love his wife as he loves himself. And a wife must respect her husband. (Ephesians 5:21-33). ERV.

That was the day I made up my mind that I will do everything in my power and by the grace of God to honour my wife as myself. This is God commandment. There should not be any compromise, any addition or water down of what God is giving as a commandment because there is a repercussion when you disobey Him on marital issue. The scriptures say, "Husbands, love you wives the same as Christ loved the church and gave his life for it. It is a commandment and not a deliberation or discussion. Likewise, wives, be willing to serve your own husbands in everything, the same as the Lord. Your husband is the head of you (the wife), just as Christ is the head of the church.

Truth be told, some wives in churches respect their pastors, priest, prophets, etc. than their husband at home. Your husband is the authority over you, (the wife) in everything. I can understand that the pastor in your church is your spiritual authority. You need to understand that the pastor too have his own wife that he must love according to the Word of God if he is true to his calling, but unfortunately there are many things happening in the body of Christ nowadays concerning marriages that is not according to Scriptures.

May I let you know that love is a choice, not a feeling. It is also a ah choice to love the other person and the choice can not be made in the context of "feeling" because those change every day. That is the reason you must understand the Word of God. The scriptures say, "You are God's dear children, so try to be like him. Live a life of love. Love others just as Christ loved us. He gave himself for us—a sweet-smelling offering and sacrifice to God. But there must be no sexual sin among you. There must not be any kind of evil or selfishly wanting more and more, because such things are not right for God's holy people.

Also, there must be no evil talk among you. Don't say things that are foolish or filthy. These are not for you. But you should be giving thanks to God. You can be sure of this: No one will have a place in the kingdom of Christ and of God if that person commits sexual sins, or does evil things, or is a person who selfishly wants more and more. A greedy person like that is serving a false god. Don't let anyone fool you with words that are not true. God gets very angry when people who don't obey him talk like that. So don't have anything to do with them. In the past you were full of darkness, but now you are full of light in the Lord. So live like children who belong to the light.

This light produces every kind of goodness, right living, and truth. Try to learn what pleases the Lord. Have no part in the things that people in darkness do, which produce nothing good. Instead, tell everyone how wrong those things are. Actually, it is shameful to even talk about the things those people do in secret. But the light makes clear how wrong those things are.

Yes, everything is made clear by the light. This is why we say, "Wake up, you who are sleeping! Rise from death, and Christ will shine on you." So be very careful how you live. Live wisely, not like fools. I mean that you should use every opportunity you have for doing good, because these are evil times. So don't be foolish with your lives, but learn what the Lord wants you to do." (Ephesians 5:1-17). ERV.

May I encourage both husband and wife that are Born Again Christian, that the most important relationship you have with your spouse is as your brother/sister in Christ Jesus. You, the husband is first and then your wife next, and again you are one in Christ Jesus. Whenever I remember that my wife is my sister in Christ Jesus, I treat her well as much as I can by His grace.

That means, to me and every husbands, according to the Scriptures that say, "Husbands, love your wives the same as Christ loved the church and gave his life for it. He died to make the church holy. He used the telling of the Good News to make the church clean by washing it with water. Christ died so that he could give the church to himself like a bride in all her beauty. He died so that the church could be holy and without fault, with no evil or sin or any other thing wrong in it. And husbands should love their wives like that.

They should love their wives as they love their own bodies. The man who loves his wife loves himself, because no one ever hates his own body, but feeds and takes care of it. And that is what Christ does for the church because we are parts of his body." (Ephesian 5:25-30). ERV. There is nowhere in Scriptures that says husbands may punch his wife, slag her off, ridicule her, torture her emotionally, physically or physiological. Or that husbands, starve your wives in basic necessity of life especially sexual needs than when you just function in the realm of "husband and wife".

I know that we will not be marrying in heaven but will know one another as brothers and sisters. Likewise, to my wife and every wives, according to the Scriptures that say, "Wives, be willing to serve your husbands the same as the Lord. A husband is the head of his wife, just as Christ is the head of the church. Christ is the Saviour of the church, which is his body. The church serves under Christ, so it is the same with you wives. You should be willing to serve your husbands in everything." (Ephesians 5:22-24). ERV.

There is nowhere in Scriptures that says, wives, you may treat your husbands like foot mat, rubbish him in the way you talk to him and disrespect him. For you are the one to wear trouser in the house as the boss. Wives, have your way all the time and if not your way, you may starve your husbands in everything especially in sexual needs until you have your way. This is not the Godly marriage that the Bible teach.

For the Scripture say, "God has chosen you and made you his holy people. He loves you. So your new life should be like this: Show mercy to others. Be kind, humble, gentle, and patient. Don't be angry with each other, but forgive each other. If you feel someone has wronged you, forgive them. Forgive others because the Lord forgave you.

Together with these things, the most important part of your new life is to love each other. Love is what holds everything together in perfect unity. Let the peace that Christ gives control your thinking. It is for peace that you were chosen to be together in one body. And always be thankful. Let the teaching of Christ live inside you richly. Use all wisdom to teach and counsel each other. Sing psalms, hymns, and spiritual songs with thankfulness in your hearts to God. Everything you say and everything you do should be done for Jesus your Lord.

And in all you do, give thanks to God the Father through Jesus. Wives, be willing to serve your husbands. This is the right thing to do in following the Lord. Husbands, love your wives, and be gentle to them." (Colossians 3:12-19). ERV. So, in that context, I believe that our relationship is an eternal one. You should treat your spouse as your brother or sister in Christ. The situation happening nowadays is that many people in church has been programmed by "modern day church" to treat church brothers and sisters in Christ so much better than their spouse.

May I say that if we could only bridge the gap so that husband and wife are brothers and sisters in Christ first. Then this could, by the grace of God, stem the tide of dissolving marriages that plagues the "Church" in recent times. I believe this is the time for believers to see their spouse as their brother or sister in Christ. You see, the principle of living with your spouse as your brother or sister in Christ is well established in Scriptures. Yes, it is true that we don't "naturally" want to die to our desire to be "happy". Yes, we don't "naturally" want to let go of our childhood programming that taught us to live life ever after.

I know that it is not that easy for you to treat your spouse as your brother or sister in Christ, I believe when you put your mind to do it by His grace! It is done. Ask for the grace of God to help you out and give you the ability that will shift your thinking to where response becomes what is natural, and not "forced". Let me use the example of John the Baptist what he said concerning Jesus Christ, that "He must decrease, so that Jesus Christ may increase". May I encourage any wife reading this book to apply the same principle or to say, the same wisdom from God toward your husband.

When you can apply this principle, you will understand that your marriage is not just about your happiness alone, but about you being conform to the image of Christ Jesus. With this, I believe both husband and wife will be able to work out how each person respond to one another in positive way. Believe me, even after 29 years of marriage, each day is an "asking for grace" day which made it better and better each day especially with 4 men in the house. That is why I thank God for my wife everyday for Godly wisdom, strength, patience and His grace to cope for all this years. My wife, I thank God for your life and I appreciate you.

I want you to understand that it will be challenging for me to love my wife as my sister in Christ without the ongoing daily (grace of God) poured out on us. Today, I can say that by that grace of God, there is a deep gratitude in our hearts of the goodness of God. May I encourage you to ask God for that grace to help you daily in your marital journey. Hear this, I believe that marital relationship is to conform you and I through the work of the Holy Spirit to the image of Christ Jesus and to further the Kingdom of God on earth. Any other goals or reasons to get married is a distant second.

May I say this, that our greatest joy and happiness should be from bending our knees at the cross daily, repenting of our selfish pride and arrogance, accepting His grace, picking up our cross and following Him. Marriage is the beautiful reflection of God relationship with His people.

I want you to take a positive stand on your marital life today even though, you may not "feel" like loving your spouse everyday, but you need to understand that the marriage God want is for you to love your spouse each day, no matter what! You know what! Making a conscious decision is what marital commitment is all about, i.e. the decision to love and the choice.

Paul said, "So I bow in prayer before the Father. Every family in heaven and on earth gets its true name from him. I ask the Father with his great glory to give you the power to be strong in your spirits. He will give you that strength through his Spirit. I pray that Christ will live in your hearts because of your faith. I pray that your life will be strong in love and be built on love.

My prayer for you is that as you are reading this book, the Holy Spirit will give you the power to understand the greatness of Christ's love—how wide, how long, how high, and how deep that love is. Christ's love is greater than anyone can ever know, but I pray that you will be able to know that love. Then you can be filled with everything God has for you." *(Ephesians 3:14-19). ERV.*

Let me encourage you on something about marriage you don't normally hear very often. You see, some say marriage is 50/50, others say 100/100. Honestly to me, the happiest marriage is 0/100, where the Lord is 100.... loving. I pray that the love of God completely 100% through your spouse, so that your spouse will begin to love you through His love. I know it is hard work but it is worth every second at the end of it all. The truth is this, when the love of God come through each of you, it will be as though whatever you may have gone through in the past is nothing compared to the joy and peace of each other company.

I want you to ask God in prayer today to speak clearly to your spouse heart what you need. I know that at times, you get on each other's nerve. You know what I mean, when your spouse drives you nuts. Maybe your spouse didn't do something you expected him or her to do, or did something you didn't expect him or her to do. You see, most of the time, you firmly believe that your annoyance is usually justifiable and sometimes you know that it's not. Sometimes you are annoyed with your spouse because your spouse failed to meet needs(to be honest) that you should really be meeting yourself.

May I be real to every married couple reading this book that, when you get married, one of the most important conversations that needs to be address or discuss is one about expectations. Truth be told, you should probably have that conversation before you even get married and revisit it often with time and life experiences. The conversation about expectation need to be address so that each person know what the other wants and expects and this will give each person a great chance to voice concerns about any of the expectations that come up.

One of the great thing about marriage is that you and I have a spouse, who is often able to meet many of our needs. One thing I will say to you is that it is a blessing and again you need to be careful about setting unreasonable expectations. The truth is that there are some needs that your spouse can't meet, and honestly, your spouse shouldn't have to.

May I discuss with you few of the marriage needs your spouse can't meet such as Emotional Peace. The truth is that when it comes to emotional peace, each person often find it by working through any baggage we may have. You see, life can dish out a lot, and when you don't work through your "stuff", the baggage begins to build. You need to understand that, no matter how much your spouse loves you, working through that "stuff" and finding the peace you desire is something you have to do on your own. The only thing your spouse can do for you is to offer support, but you have to do the work.

Let me mention the needs of Happiness that is very crucial in any marriage. May I say, shouldn't your spouse make you happy? Of course, they should. However, the happiness you feel from being with your spouse should be the icing on the cake. Truth be told, the person you marry cannot be your source of happiness. The process of finding happiness in life is something you have to figure out on your own. Expecting your spouse to supply your happiness is a dangerous move. I believe God is the only source of Happiness.

Let me share the aspect of spirituality with you that your spouse can't meet. I believe that there should be a Spiritual connection with your spouse, but only God can meet the spiritual needs everyone have within. May I encourage you, if you feel empty or lost, and you are seeking a deeper connection to help you find solid ground, turn to the Source who is Jesus Christ. Accept Him today as your Lord and Saviour. Invite Him into your life so that He may fill you with His Spirit.

I know your life will not be the same again, and that is where you will find what you need to build yourself. Ultimately, I know that with God being in the centre of your marriage, you will build a great marital relationship with your spouse. It is very important that in your marital relationship, you need to be feeling fulfilled. Let me ask you if there is something missing, don't automatically turn to your spouse to fill that gap. For instance, are you happy with your career? Is there a dream you want to pursue? Are you involve with your friends, families or involved at church?

Yes, your marriage should be very fulfilling, but it cannot be your only source of fulfilment. You need to find out what's really missing from your life, and start filling any void with things that can add meaning to your life.

Truth about Marriage you must know. Sex is a gift from God. Explore it.

Most churches and parents don't want to talk about SEX, but unfortunately it is the area that we are shy to talk about that many people especially the church people failed big time. The church and parents must speak out more on these issue to their youths and unmarried people that they don't have any business to do with sex until they are married.

This is the generation that Youth Pastors and Parents must help to eradicate teenagers pregnancy especially in church. These youths must be educated to abstain from sexual activities until they are mature enough, get married and start a family life. Churches and Parents must make their youths and young adults understand the hardship and difficulty of being a single parent at an early age.

I do understand that children are blessings from the Lord but I will advice you to wait for the right time when you are ready to start having your children with your own husband or wife. Many youths had make the mistake of having a child as a teenager or a boy impregnated a teenager girl which will eventually turns out to be regrets, hardship and struggling for many years to come.

The truth of these situation is that, it is the girl that will suffer most of the time. For instance, she may not be able to complete her education when other are completing. In most cases, she will drop out of school and at the end of the day, the father of the child will marry someone else.

The unfortunate situation is that the girl will be struggling to make ends meet if her parents or the boy parent are not there to support her and the baby. Listen educate your youths that there is nothing like girl meet boy. Girl fall in love with the boy and get pregnant. Let me be real with you, it is the girl that will eventually miss out and continued to struggle in life.

The truth I want you to understand is that, this is the generation that the church and the home must work together so that Satan (the god of this world) must be stopped, selling lies to define sex to our children and teenagers. The church and the parents must educate their children in the right way on sex.

If not, the society we live and the school system will educate them in the wrong direction. Nowadays the average child is expose to pornography at age 11. I know that many parents are not comfortable to talk about sex with their children at an early age.

The problem on this is that many of us wait until our children are teenagers before we start to talk to them about sex. Unfortunately many of them may have been taught about sex in the way you may not have imagined. The world and the education system will teach boys to use condom and the girls to take morning after pills.

At this point, may I tell you that you are not building any foundation for sex education anymore but fighting to destroy a foundation that Satan (the god of this world) has already built. And this is a big fight for many parents to win. I pray that God will help you win the heart and soul of your children back to God.

May I encourage every parent to take a stand of this issue, and if you don't educate your children about sex in the right way, society will educate them the wrong way. A wrong understanding of sex education among our young people is robbing them of a bright future and destroying our nation. That is why we have to educate them on sex before it is too late.

I believe that sex is a beautiful gift created by God for a man and woman that have vowed to spend the rest of their life together as husband and wife. You need to enjoy this gift of God to the full as husband and wife and not with anyone else that is not your spouse.

Over the years, many people have allow Satan to use this gift of God in a negative way to mess up their children, marriage and family due to ignorance and lack of understanding of the importance and purpose of sex. They have allowed this gift of God to be a bad word because it has not been used as it should especially those that are not married.

Many youths that grew up in church environment were not taught about sex education because it is a taboo word to mention among church folks. The truth for many youths in church is that their framework for sex was built by friends at school and the social media.

Let me encourage every husband and wife to enjoy their sex life to the maximum apart from the medical reasons. Don't allow the cloud of lies formed during your teenager years about sex to rob you off from enjoying your sex life with your spouse. As a Child of God, take back the gift of sex in your marriage and let it be a positive word.

You need to explore the gift of sex in marriage for a healthy sexual relationship as a married couple regularly. Use your sex life in marriage with your spouse to enjoy sexual intimacy. Apart from having your children, use your sex life to distress and enjoy it to the full.

I want you to understand what the Scriptures say about sex outside of marital relationship as "sexual immorality" (1 Corinthians 7:2), therefore sex can only be considered healthy if it done between husband and wife that have vowed to live together as God ordained.

The Scriptures is very specific about sexual immorality because marriage is a requirement for healthy sexual intimacy between husband and wife. For the Scriptures say, "But because of the temptation to sexual immorality, each man should have his own wife and each woman her own husband. The husband should give to his wife her conjugal rights, and likewise the wife to her husband.

For the wife does not have authority over her own body, but the husband does. Likewise the husband does not have authority over his own body, but the wife does. Do not deprive one another, except perhaps by agreement for a limited time, that you may devote yourselves to prayer; but then come together again, so that Satan may not tempt you because of your lack of self-control."(1 Corinthians 7:2-5).

Chapter 5
Outside Influence.
Who Are You Listening To?

You are to be aware that not everyone you know is a supporter of you marriage, even if they support you individually. The most important people in your marital relationship is the two of you, i.e., you and your spouse, and not your friends, your mum and dad or your co-workers.

Let me be real with you and say it as it should! Seek out friends of your marriage by defining what a real friend is, such as a friend that do not give you a hall pass or seek the easy way out; instead he or she hold you accountable. A friend that don't judge, but keeping an open yet helpful mind is key. True friends do not run and gossip about your deepest secrets. True friend will pray for your marriage.

May I suggest that regardless of how close you are to your family or friends, be careful of what you share with them. Be very considerate of the motives of those outside your marriage. In blended families, outside influence can even include the other biological parent outside the home, so be aware of this fact.

You need to realise that outside influence can be absolute toxic to any marriage. So, these are some of the things you must guard against that will make your marriage strong, that is;

(A) Keep your business between you and your spouse.

(B) Bring professional and true friends of your marriage into the picture, but only when necessary.

(C) Do not allow the people around you to see cracks in the foundation on your marriage.

(D) Do no be phoney, but do keep your issues behind closed doors.

(E) Considering finding a mentoring couple that has a truly successful marriage. This should be a couple that you can both speak to when issue arise.

(F) Exercise compromise and sacrifice in your marital relationship, so can be better equipped to handle major issues between the two of you.

The Right Ways to Treat your Spouse Better.

I know that you've heard it before that, "you reap what you sow" and some people may believe that it is true and some may not believe it. To me, I believe that if you want to achieve something good in life, you should give something back to achieve it maybe money, time, endurance etc.

Therefore, however you want your spouse to treat you good, that is how you need to treat your spouse in the first place. For instance, if you want your spouse to respect you, respect him or her first. Don't belittle , name calling or mistreat your spouse especially when other people are present.

Similarly, don't engage in disrespectful behaviour such as staying out all night, or acting as if you are single. The truth of the whole matter is that, you respect yourself first and other people will give you the respect you deserve.

I believe that it is not only the wife that needs compliments from the husband. Husbands too need to receive compliments from their wife such as, "you are looking good dude and smell nice" Such simple compliments will make any man head to swell and his chest expand. It is good to compliment each other.

There are simple compliments that husband and wife need to compliment one another such as a well done chore around the house or just by saying how much you appreciate one another. It goes a long way when you appreciate one another to create a conducive and peaceful atmosphere in the home than not appreciating at all.

Husband and wife must help one another when needed or when you know that your partner needs helping. Don't wait for him or her to ask you before you help. After all you always render help to somebody outside of your home without them asking for help to prove you are a gentle man or a nice lady.

Always treat your spouse as you want to be treated, and don't assume that it is your spouse duty or chores in the house. That does not mean that when you are less busy, you will not help him or her to do the chores when you are less busy. When you see something to be done around the house, just do it without making a big deal out of the situation.

As I have mentioned earlier, if you want to be treated well, treat your spouse well first. It is just like if you want intimacy with your spouse, be intimate with him or her first. For instance if your spouse is not very intimate as you like, I suggest that you initiate ways to be very intimate with him or her and it does not always have to be sex.

Intimacy can me touching, hugging, caressing, cuddling and holding hands. A good shoulder or back rub works well too and you can help your spouse to have a good foot massage and it works well also.

I believe that the frequency of this type of affections will be contagious and become normal practice to both of you. Let me encourage every husband and wife that if you want your spouse to trust you, be trustworthy. Trust in marriage does not always have to do with infidelity.

In marriage, it is important that you trust your spouse especially with money, kids and major decision about your family. The truth is that, in order to gain each others trust, you need to be active in everything regarding your marriage and don't leave all decision to your spouse.

May I say this that, if you want your spouse to trust you, even with your past infidelity reasons, you must be true to yourself, by not engaging in untrustworthy behaviours anymore. I believe that if you communicate your needs with your spouse at all times, sometimes action with words help a person learn a new behaviour.

Habits that will help you to be Happily Married.

Many people don't believe that happy marriage do exist. It might have something to do with our upbringing or our thinking that a happy married couple doesn't experience or go through any changes or stressful situations.

What I will be revealing to you in this book is for you to know how you can handle those stressful situation in your marital life that will make a difference between you and most other couples that are not experiencing happiness in their marriage.

To be honest with you, everyone definition of what constitutes as a happy marriage may vary. In my opinion, a happily married couple is one who loves being married and is always willing to do whatever is necessary to maintain that happiness.

May I encourage you to adopt these habits that will help you to live happily in your marital relationship with your spouse. To each individual, you need to adopt specific habits that will work for you as a married man or woman for success in your marriage. You must understand that:

(A) Couples that communicate the triumphs, defeats and unpleasant situations together stay together. The best marital relationships are those that both stay as husband and wife that are completely honest as well as receptive to feedback. Both couple can easily apologise to each other, with the word. "I'm sorry love".

This is a good relationship that you need to adopt where neither the husband or the wife is not afraid to voice out his or her opinion and both of them are equally willing to listen even when one or both of them are at fault. It create strong bond between husband and wife, and it works all the time, trust me.

(B) Husband and wife take responsibility for their action. In the type of partnership like this, there will not be a great deal of finger pointing or shifting blame. There is internal honesty with husband and wife who is not afraid to face their own demons and transform. The transformation is where many fall short. Your spouse deserves the absolute best of you. This is a stunning statement! But it is true.

(C) Husband and wife that do something differently in their marriage stay together. Let me explain, because to this couple, they understand that certain behaviours will not help or benefit their relationship. So, they collectively choose different options.

They are able to understand the consequence or repercussion of wrong decision and the cost of poor judgement. They quickly embrace and recognise that if it is not good for one, it can not happen around them.

(D) Husband and wife that express love as often as possible stays together. You need to demonstrate your love to one another in the form of touch, praise and affirmations. Let me say this that couple that never neglect to show love especially during hard time or challenges stay together.

(E) Husband and wife that pray and worship God together stay together. I believe that your marriage will stand the test of time with a Spiritual connection. A couple that prays together, live happily together. Hear this, being "happily married" is not an anomaly.

Everyone have the potential to experience the exact same joy. It will not come by chance. When you show up with your everything, it makes the huge impact. Everyone can share this same level of peace, love and happiness when we are willing to make the needed sacrifice.

Chapter 6
Ways To Touch Your Spouse All Day Long.

I thank God for His grace and mercy upon my marital relationship with my wife for the past 29 years. To God be the glory! Amen. Today, I can say that a happy marital relationship requires prayer, hard work on the relationship, lot of patience, a good measure of tolerance in all while trying to figure this other person out.

Real talk! there is going to be bumps on the road and also there are going to be some great moments that you going to share with another person. The truth is that, it has clearly been one of the best decisions I've ever made, marrying my wife.

All that being said! May I ask you, how do you keep the home fires burning, that spark of romance going and a hint of mystery in the air? I believe that just a simple, unexpected touch every now and again with your spouse matters significantly in a happy marital relationship.

For instance, not a grope or caress but more like a gentle stroke, a whisper in the ear, or a flirtation wink will always help for a conducive atmosphere. Sometimes your wife may be annoyed with you (the husband) in the way you are caressing her. Whether you the (husband) is doing it with the palm of your hand or caressing that seem to be a turn on for you but unfortunately, it is a turn off for her.

The truth is that, most women may not be entirely turned off by her husband desire to touch her. But she may be turned off by the fact that the only time he touched her is to tell her "let's get it on". The signal he gave to let her know he wanted to be physical intimate just serve as a reminder to her that most of the time, there were anything but............

The situation of the above mentioned couple is not rear at all nowadays. The reality is that many couples don't touch each other all day, all week and still expect to feel the connection to one another when the light go out.

The truth is this that we can not neglect one another as husband and wife all day and expect to feel passion at the end of it. Passion and intimacy has to be built, starting first thing in the morning. In many ways, we need to essentially be "making love" to our spouse all day.

You may ask! How can I make love all day when I have other commitment such as my job, kids, household responsibilities etc. I believe that it is not so hard as it seems. Remember those early days in your marriage of not being able to keep your hands off each other?

You can start to feel that way again by the he of God by making it a point of duty not to keep your hands off each other. May I say that if all day feels like foreplay, the transition into the bed room will be a much more natural. It's easier to keep a fire going that already lit than to start a new one from scratch.

One of the ways to touch your spouse all day long is to walk to your spouse and give him or her a bear hug. Say to your spouse that, (It is well. Whatever we are going through, I got your back and I love you). Another way, (especially for the wife) is to sit on your husband lap or you may cuddle next to him when watching tv or film. This will get both of you close to one another.

On the next aspect of ways to touch your spouse all day long is very easy to do. This is to hold hands while you walk in public to say, "I am proud of whom my spouse is". In London, England, it is a common practice for old couples to hold hands in public and I love it when I see one.

Another simple way to get close to your spouse is to rest your hand on his or her knee while you talk. The truth is that this always make the other person to listen attentively. You see, all this ways is to make every wife feel comfortable and beautiful within because it is true.

Let me go further to the bedroom scenario. As a wife, when in bed with your husband, you lay your head on his chest and rub his tummy. Trust me your husband will feel like a king in his castle and you as the queen of that castle.

Truth be told, most men grow up in the environment that they don't see or experience open affection. It will be very challenging to those type of men to practice or engage in what they don't know or have the experience in their years of growing up. They only watch it on televising or films.

May I encourage you to make up your mind today and begin to put this into action immediately by touching your spouse showing love towards one another so that you can keep your marriage afresh. I believe that you will love being loved.

There are some habits I have developed over the years such as giving my wife a kiss before I leave home each day. I know it is a good habit for husband and wife to practice. Even during the day time that are together, you can kiss your spouse on the back of the neck, or forehead kiss or on the cheek for no reason other than your expression of love towards your husband or wife.

I do appreciate my wife so much especially when she gave me a shoulder or back rub and I do likewise for her to release the tension from the body and it works. You may also give foot massage to ease the foot tension. Do simple task for one another such as greasing your spouse scalp, lotion his or her back, etc.

May I encourage you to do those little tasks that made a difference that will help your marriage successful such as putting your arm around your spouse shoulder while you sit next to each other.

You need to pick at least two things from the list I have shared with you and begin to practice them from today. I guarantee you that there will be a change for better in your marital relationship with your spouse.

Unspoken Rules About Marriage That Speaks Volume.

When a man and a woman are getting married, they took wedding vows and meant every word plan to love, honour and respect one another til881 death do them part. It is a spoken promise to the husband and wife, and we can call them rules, really!

This is to say, "these are the rules we plan to play and base the relationship upon so that things can work out better as planned". Being married to my wife for quite a while, life has thrown a few curve balls our way. I've learnt to be flexible and we've put through all the unexpected things life can throw at us such as bad investment, redundancy etc.

The truth is that my wife and I have managed everything life can throw at us pretty well. One of the things I have realised is that even with many years of marital experience, there are still some rules we follow that are unspoken.

I believe that these are the rules that have been rooted in my wife upbringing as her family values and we are able to follow them with ease. For us it worked brilliantly. And oddly enough, despite not needing to talk about this stuff, these rules are at the core of what makes our marriage work.

Let me share with you some of the unspoken rules about marriage. I pray that you are able to determine what your unspoken rules are and they serve your marriage well in Jesus name. On this unspoken rules in marriage, you need to make time to connect with your spouse.

Nowadays, technology is a crucial part of our lives, and that's fine until we begin to let it consume our life. Even when you are in a job that requires you to be connected all the time. May I suggest that you find a way to intentionally unplug so that you can reconnect with your spouse because your family matters.

One of the unspoken rules in marriage that you need to understand for you to enjoy your marriage is that you don't critique your spouse's family or friends. Your spouse family or friends have known your spouse before your spouse knows you. Believe me, no good thing come out from saying negative things to your spouse about those people he or she love before you came along.

The truth is that your spouse already sees the same issue you saw anyway and there is no reason for you to come along and make it worse that it is. Hear this, unless your spouse specifically ask for your opinion, keep the criticism to yourself and yourself only. If not you will make more enemies than friends among your spouse family and friends.

Another issue of unspoken rules about marriage that is common among those people that have married for some time is the situation of bringing up old issues that need to have been forgotten long tome ago. May I suggest to you that when a situation is in the past and have already been discussed and settled, please leave it.

Using old situation, argument of the past issue to make your point or to make your spouse feel bad in marriage is not going to do either of you any good. It is not a healthy way of communication for a good marriage that will sustain the test of time.

You need to choose your battle carefully and may I say that must understand that not every battle is worth fighting. Be wise to choose the battle that are worth fighting for and leave the other stuff alone.

To be honest, I do not think that arguments will not happen in your relationship with your spouse. Yes, it will happen. What you must know is that if you need to argue, please do so with respect to one another.

Always remember that you don't bring up painful situations, using harsh or foul languages and just being mean to one another will not get you heard. It definitely does not help your marriage at all.

May I say that if you want to have a good marital relationship, please do not make empty threats or say certain nasty things to one another. For example, if you have no intention of getting a divorce, don't threating your spouse by saying it.

Know that making empty threats to get your points across to your spouse causes pain. It put you in a position where your spouse does not trust and take you serious any more.

Another aspect of unspoken rules about marriage that I will suggest to you is that you keep the world out of your marriage business because not every dirty linen we expose to the sun. There is no need of you telling everybody include your mother and your mother in-law every time you have an argument with your spouse.

The truth is that, if you keep reporting your husband to everyone you know, I want you to remember that the whole world will always see your spouse through the negative lens you have provided since they don't get to experience all the good stuff your spouse have done.

Hear this, what make me strong for my marriage with my wife is that I cherish my friendship with her and this friendship is the core of our union. May I encourage you to begin now if you have not been cherishing your friendship with your spouse because if you neglect it your marriage will suffer.

This is one of the best thing you can do for your marriage so that you can enjoy a successful marital life. Don't make assumption, it never work as far as marital relationship in concerned. Good communication in marriage is very important and assumption is often the wrong thing to do. May I say that instead of you guessing what is in your spouse mind or what his/her intention is, please just ask!

Chapter 7
Huge Mistakes to Avoid In Marriage.

It is true that we all make mistakes one way or the other, but some are more detrimental than others. When we mistake, we never feel good. We felt dejected and terrible especially when we made a wrong decision which needed to have been avoided in the first place and then come with regrettable repercussion.

The problem that is harder to deal with than the mistakes is the impact it causes and not just on our personal level but the impact it bring on the people we love most, i.e. our spouse or children.

The truth is, there is no perfect marriage. Conflict occur in the house and mistakes are made and that does not mean that your marriage is in trouble. If there is anything I would suspect is those married couples that claim that there has been no mistakes. They are the one 's in trouble.

One of the aspect of marriage mistakes to avoid, whether you are newly married or you have married for a long time is the fact that mistakes or challenge will happen. But make use of whatever mistake or challenge as a learning curve and try as much as possible to correct it or avoid it next time.

I believe that some of the mistakes or challenges we have as couples may be avoided, while others are simply the result of moving through life and managing the unexpected. To be honest, most of the time, we don't always make the right call.

This book is to help you avoid costly mistakes that may damage your marriage. It is true that you learn by making mistakes but try as much as possible not to make the huge mistake that may cost you dearly. As I've said before, there is no mistake free marriage.

However, when it comes to mistakes, there are some that can be avoided if we give it a thorough true thought. For instance, making an important decision when you are angry or frustrated, is not a good idea in marriage.

One of the huge mistakes to avoid in marriage is for you not to honour your word. Let your word be your bond. If you say you are going to do something, make sure that you do it positively. For any relationship to work well, both parties must honour their words.

For every married couple, you have already promised your spouse to be faithful from the beginning. Why are you know stepping out of line and breaking promises? This is one of the huge mistake to avoid in marriage because it will always be referred to, when there is argument with one of you many years down the line.

Let me share with you this huge mistake to avoid in your marriage for you not to disrespect your spouse. It is good for husband and wife to respect one another at all times. This does not mean that you agree to every ideas and decision your spouse make even when you know that it is wrong. It really means that you respect your spouse more than anyone outside your family.

The issue of complete neglecting oneself as a married man or woman is a big mistake to do. Can I say this that each person in marital relationship is responsible for his or her self-care. What you must always remember is that you are attracted to your spouse in the first place before you the relationship started.

So, let your spouse still see that attractiveness in you, no matter of the years you have married. What I want you to understand is to take excellent care of yourself mentally, physically, emotionally and spiritually. This will help you in many areas of life especially in your marriage to have a good relationship with your spouse.

Another huge mistake you must avoid in your marriage is to put your career before your marital relationship. I can understand that pursuing your career is important, I get that. It is the way of making a living and can also be linked to your deepest passion.

However, I firmly believe that your marriage and family will suffer when you make your career the priority above your marriage and family all the time. This is because there will be times when you will be working long hours and the hustle is harder than usual, even then, you spouse should feel like your marriage comes first.

This is to everyone in marital relationship that don't show appreciation to their spouse. It is not a good idea to undermine your spouse. The truth is that one thing we all have in common is the need to feel appreciated. Your spouse may not be perfect, but it is a huge mistake not to appreciate one another even for the little task done around the house

The Role of a Purposeful Wife.

This is to affirm every wife of purpose that one of your role is to smother your husband with love. You are to love your own husband by spending time with him, being verbal and active in how you demonstrate your commitment to him. Your girlfriend is now your wife and your boyfriend is now your husband.

The truth is that as the titles change, your duties and tasks changes also. Your responsibilities and expectation change as well and for this, each household is different. Your friend or neighbour will not have the same expectation of you or you of them. It's personal between you and your spouse.

I can understand that it is not always an easy task to be the spouse of purpose you desire to be, but I believe that more efforts and energy are both required which many wives don't always possess. I know that most wife have a lot on their plate as per career wise and children, so time at hand is limited.

However, with all that is been said, you need to make the time and release more energy within you because you need your marriage to succeed. I am here to encourage you to be passionate about your marriage and all that good marital relationship possess such as a lasting partnership and true love.

Marital relationship fulfils our need to feel love and share our lives with someone who contribute to many part of our living and family life. In a good relationship, you will have an awesome feeling of commitment and connection with your spouse.

Hear this, if you love your spouse, no matter what comes your way, you will be able to take care of one another without any of you thinking otherwise. Let me say this, that, sharing your life with your spouse who cares so much about what is happening in your world is a blessing.

I believe that you have so much to be grateful for! I thank God for your life because it make sense to me that you have a goal of being the best wife possible as you desire. Obviously, there are more roles you need to play on your part that will make you as unique as possible for the wife you desire to be.

One of the roles you must be engage into is to always pray for your husband first to be the man God created him to be, as he is the priesthood over your home. May I say that praying over your marriage and family must be one of your goals as an uncommon wife attributes.

As an uncommon wife, ask God to increase your faith and that of your spouse in commitment and connection. Part of your role is to love your spouse with everything you got. Loving with everything such as carving out time for date night together, making sure that your communication is open and honest.

Let truth be told, that your intimacy with your spouse is actively alive and top on the list. Your role as a good wife is not to judge what that does make sense to you but to seek understanding for what you have questions about!

For instance, when your husband starts behaving funny or you sense that something is not right. Then you need to ask appropriate questions and do not jump to conclusion because your conclusion may go wrong. You will have yourself to blame for complicating matters worse than it was originally.

A purposeful woman will become a wife of little or no regret all the days of her marital life. As a purposeful wife that you are, you are to communicate with the king in your husband and he will respond to the queen in you. Do not take your husband for granted at any time or neglect him.

This is an essential wisdom for a woman of purpose that want to live a purposeful marital lifestyle to practice. I pray that your husband will continued to love and cherish you more without regret all the days of your life till death do you part in Jesus name. May I say that being a good wife, better still, a great wife should be part of your plan as a married woman.

As a married woman, you must know that one of your crucial goal of your marital commitment is to love your husband unconditional and no matter what! My prayer is that your husband love you with the love of the Lord and see His beauty on you daily as a precious jewel.

One of the challenges most married women face nowadays is that they do not know how to express their love to their husband apart from the bedroom. Let your husband feel love and let him know frequently that you are proud of him as a good husband and good father to your children.

May I say that being a good wife, better still, being a great wife should be lifestyle for you as a purposeful wife and a mother. I believe that as a purposeful wife, you are of the sovereign God who's redemption of you gives great purpose to every facet of your life.

I pray that from this time of your marital life, to parenting and home making, you will strive to do all things for His glory. God grace will be sufficient for you each day and His sovereignty that give you purpose will give you strength and healing especially to your pain so that you can be more encouraging and enriching to your husband every time.

Chapter 8
Changing Your Perspectives Can Change Your Marriage For The Best.

O bviously, our view of the world is what we hold to be true. Unfortunately, our perceived truths can cause us to be judgemental, jaded and detached. Over the course of our lives, our perceived truths provide numerous opportunities for us to accumulate a ship yard filled the carnage from a lifetime of wrecked relationships, friendships and partnerships.

The truth is that our perception may cause havoc in our marriage. I believe certainly that you have the power to change the trajectory of your relationship by transforming your perceptions.

May I encourage you to evaluate your behaviour and re access your commitment to your relationships. You need to change your focus from negative to positive and move from blame to ownership.

You must be accountable for your thoughts, words and action. Then stop justifying and making excuses for your destructive marriage conduct if you want to have a successful marital lifestyle.

May I say that in order to have the relationship you really want, you need to stop denying the role you play in contributing to the demise of your marriage and become courageously truthful in acknowledging and accep5ing responsibility for the state of your marital life.

I believe that changing your individual perceptions empower you to attain the marital lifestyle you desire. Let me encourage you with some attributes and values that will help you to possess and consistently implement to change your perception of your spouse and relationships.

One of the attributes and values to share with you is Honesty. You must be honest with yourself and your spouse about your wants, needs and expectations. What you must understand is that if you are not honest with yourself in addition to not openly communicating with your spouse, frustration, fear, resentment, disappointment, jealousy and anger become prevalent emotions that covertly and overtly dictate your actions in your marriage.

Successful married coupled have learned to create a safe environment in which their spouse can be honest without fear of scorn, shame or retribution.

Another attribute and value you need to understand in your marriage is Trust. It is impossible to build and sustain a relationship without the foundation of trust. I believe that trust is the bloodline of a relationship. Trust is what secures the bond that holds the structure in place. Successful couples consistently show up for their spouse in ways that display they can be trusted in good and bad times.

Commitment is another attribute and value I want to share with you. You have to be willing to engage yourself as a professional in your marital relationship. One thing each husband and wife must realise is that they must agree that their relationship is bigger than they are individually.

When good things of life happens, problems arise. Internal and external forces attack your marriage. It is on this situation that husband and wife must view these obstacles as challenges which they need to work through and overcome together as one.

May I challenge you as a husband or wife reading this book that are very serious in honouring your marriage and that you are creating the plan for success! By committing to do whatever possible it takes to maintain a healthy marital relationship with your spouse.

Both husband and wife must encourage one another at all times so that they can realise that they have the ability to choose to be fully presentable in a positive way as a married couple. Both husband and wife must realise and understand that they are empowered to choose how they communicate with, respond to, and interact with their partner.

You have to be more considerate and compassionate especially towards your spouse in every situation and circumstance. Both of you as husband and wife must be more often willing and able to make more inclusive choices for yourself, your spouse and the marriage as a whole.

I believe that with my experience and understanding of successful marital lifestyle, accountability is important for any marriage to succeed. Obviously, may I say that being accountable for your thoughts, words and actions make you more self aware and more trust worthy towards your spouse.

The truth is this, mistakes will happen and bad choices will be made as we are human. However acknowledging a negative behaviour or bad choice and taking action to correct it make your spouse feel that you are concerned about the situation. That means a lot because you cherish and value your marriage.

The next nugget I am sharing with you now is very much important to make you success in your marriage. Both husband and wife that have share vision for their marriage and that operate with one accord, their outcomes are typically achieved.

You must understand that husband and wife that achieve success in their marital life establish rules and set measureable marital goals that enhance and strengthen their marriage. Proper alignment of beliefs, values and goals helps husband and wife successfully navigate the rocky and sometimes unpredictable terrain that marriage present.

Every married couple need to understand that husband and wife that operates with integrity resolve to live intentionally and love purposefully. They view their relationship from a perspective wholeness. These couples hold them self and their spouse in high regards. As such they make decisions from a place of respect for them self and their spouse.

You must understand that for you to have a good marriage, you must remain aware and fully present in your relationship and it requires daily engagement. Husband and wife must be vigilant to understand their spouse because this will help both parties to avoid unnecessary misunderstanding.

I believe that being aware means foregoing your need, to be correct and to defend. It means completely releasing yourself to be fully immersed in the moment with your spouse as you work to recognise and appreciate what your spouse is expressing to you. Being aware requires alertness, focus and selflessness.

For you to enjoy your marriage to the full, you must be attune with your spouse by showing a sense of connection and a degree of understanding in your interaction whether verbal or non verbal that displays that you are completely in tune with one another. Atonement is the ultimate level of a married couples heart, mind, body and soul collaboration.

I believe that husband and wife that lovely and wilfully practice these values daily will definitely reach a state of marriage euphoria. With this, the energy is positive, sparks fly, passion is present and you become very open to learning and discovering new things about yourself, your spouse and taking your marital relationship to a higher level.

May I let you know that the rose coloured glasses that you wear in the beginning of your marital life can indeed become a permanent accessory in your marriage.

Love lies that ruin most marriages!

I believe that the reason there are failures, disappointment, betrayal, frustration and on going conflict too often in marriage is because people are collisional, faulty beliefs and love lies that we inherit. It may lead to marriage ruins.

One of the love lies is this that "the kids should be the centrepiece of the marriage" The truth is that, if we are not mindful, the children will be the focus of all our attention and energy while marriage takes second seat and can easily get neglected.

Over time, there will be less and less quality time spent enjoying each other's company. Without the kids, sex may be easily become uncommon commodity in the home. The truth of this situation is that the "Soul" of such relationship is starving and it is thirsty for nourishment.

May I encourage you to keep the well-being of your marital life at the centre of your focus if you want to enjoy your marriage even though, your children also benefit. Your children will actually buoyed and energise by the existence of a visible healthy love connection between you and your spouse. It create stability where your children can be at ease and feel secure.

Love Lie: He should already know!

May I ask you? What should he already know, according to wives? My husband should already know without us having to ask him what we want him to do, especially around the house or in relation to the children.

Hear this; he should already know my likes and dislikes (as I may tell you that these certainly changes) without you telling him. The truth is that many times, you think that if he does not know, you falsely conclude that he doesn't care, he doesn't love you enough or less invested in the marriage or the children. In turn, you can become resentful.

May I say that you have to realise that men are made differently, think differently and are wired differently. What you must understand is that your husband probably does not know and this does not mean the end of the world. It does not mean that your husband is uncaring. You need to be direct and specific with your husband and get good at asking.

Love Lies: Longevity means that the relationship is deeply satisfying, fulfilling and juicy.

Let's talk! For many years we have been hearing married couples mentioning the longevity of their marriage and if the numbers of the years is 20 years or more, we automatically say "Congratulations". We tend to automatically equate longevity of the marriage with the quality of the relationship.

However, with my own experience in marital counselling, I know that husband and wife may have been married for many years and can still experienced constant frustration with more pain than pleasure. The reason for that situation is that the marriage is "dry" instead of "juicy". May I tell you that a juicy marriage is one where both husband and wife are deeply satisfied and fulfilled.

Chapter 9
Divorce Is Not An Option.
You Can Protect Your Marriage.

I feel saddened whenever I hear about any husband and wife experiencing challenges in their marriage. That is why I made it my primary focus or desire to help couples before they arrive at this ugly decision of divorce.

What I want you to know is that my work with relationships is not base only on couples who are happily married because they actually still care for their relationship with their spouse and are willing to do what is necessary to maintain that feeling.

My heart bleeds when I see husband and wife tearing one another apart. They tend to destroy everything they have labour to built together for many years. Divorce is against the plan of God for marriage institution. God hate divorce.

It is the true that God hate divorce and there are reasons for that which I will share with you accordingly. The unfortunate situation to most husband and wife that goes through separation, is that by the time they seek for help, divorce is imminent and become the very real option.

What I want you to understand is that, the thoughts of divorce and conversation on separation will immediately alter the behaviour of both partners and affect the efforts put forth. The moment those words are used, things change.

Let me encourage every husband and wife to love one another more each day as they navigate through the most difficult period of marriage challenges. This is the period that you need to be selective with your words and still be able to speak life into your relationship.

I know that shooting is easy in marriage, but it takes a truly committed husband or wife to stay and fight for their marriage. For you as the husband or wife, you must change your mind-set to remain in a proactive mode, instead of a reactive one. Waiting to take action after you've arrived at your breaking point is risky.

Let me share with you some of the reasons couples divorce so that you don't fall into that situation. I will be discussing in this chapter how you can protect your marriage and have a successful marital lifestyle. One of the most common reason is:

Infidelity or Someone Cheated.

Infidelity (also referred to as cheating, adultery, or having an affair) is a violation of a couple's assumed or stated contract regarding emotional and/or sexual exclusivity. Other scholars define infidelity as the subjective feeling that one's partner has violated a set of rules or relationship norms; this violation results in feelings of sexual jealousy and rivalry.

What constitutes an act of infidelity is dependent upon the exclusivity expectations within the relationship. In marital relationships, exclusivity expectations are commonly assumed although they are not always met. When they are not met, research has found that psychological damage can occur, including feelings of rage and betrayal, lowering of sexual and personal confidence, and damage to self-image.

Depending on the context, men and women can experience social consequences if their act of infidelity becomes public. The form and extent of these consequences are often dependent on the gender of the unfaithful person. One measure of infidelity among couples is the frequency of children secretly conceived with a different partner, leading to "non-paternities". Such covertly illegitimate children amount to about 1-2% of all new-borns in Western populations.

The truth is that when someone in the marriage has broken the trust, that journey towards recovery will have its share of twists and turns. However, it isn't impossible. Couple have to be honest during the rebuilding process, once they actually choose to rebuild. Of course, there is no hurt like the pain that surfaces from someone betraying your trust and being careless with your heart. Truth be told, not every marriage is infidelity safe. There are individuals who don't know or care to be faithful.

May I encourage those that are faithful in their relationship with their spouse about their wants, needs and desires. Whenever you are not being fulfilled, being vocal and realistic (as loving as possible), I want you to understand that it will provide an opportunity for your spouse to correct and deliver. On the other hand when you are not doing the fulfilling for your spouse needs (without making any excuses), you must step up your spousal game up as well and take excellent care of the half of the marriage.

Don't Allow Divorce become a very Real Option!

Let me warn both husbands and wives not to tosses that ugly word "divorce" around at any time in your marriage because it will set the tone for your relationship future. The truth is that if you say it, you are letting your spouse know it has been considered.

In some cases, it will give your spouse permission to throw in the towel. I can understand that no one will want to put forth the energy or effort to be in a partnership with someone who does not appear to be committed. The truth is, we must ask our self if we've personally done everything required to save our marriage prior to arriving at the thought of divorce.

Again, you need not to use that word "divorce" during arguments or when you are frustrated is the key. One thing that I do understand in marital relationships is that it is irresponsible of anyone to say negative things he or she don't mean without considering the impact it may have on the marriage. So, think deeply before you say somethings concerning your marriage.

There are warning signs which must not be ignored.

The truth is, if you smell smoke, look for the fire and take emergency action. You can not afford to pretend as though an issue doesn't exist. Sleeping in separate rooms, not communicating and not being intimate for weeks on end are red-hot signs something is seriously wrong.

Out of experience, I can tell you that a marriage can not live if the partners are dead towards one another. You can not be afraid to lovingly acknowledge and discuss your issues as a couple. Ask your spouse how both of you can be better in your relationship towards each other, making sacrifices and taking action that are all necessary.

Forgiveness is non-existent

Truth be told, we all make mistakes continuously. Since we are not perfect, we tend to make lousy decisions. I want you to understand that deciding to forgive your spouse, yet reliving and reminding him or her their mistakes constantly is counter productive. Not only does it keep the negative memory fresh in your mind, it pushes your partner even further away.

Not many people would choose to remain in a situation where they are regularly considered the villain. I want you to understand that forgiveness does not erase the error, it simply proves the commitment was strong enough to survive.

Apologizing is hard work. You know what else is hard? Forgiving an apologizing spouse.

Why? Why should that be hard? Well, for one, it's easy to suspect that the apology isn't sincere ("I'm sorry." "You are not!"). For another, when this isn't the first argument on a certain misbehaviour, the wounded party sees a trend and fears it will continue indefinitely. Am I enabling more of this bad behaviour? For another, staying angry gives you emotional leverage. For another, staying wounded gives you the moral high ground in future negotiations. Your injury is an asset--why would you give away this form of capital?

Let me tell you that holding onto anger, however, poisons your soul. It marinates your spirit in toxins that will affect everything else in your life and especially in this most important of all your human relationships. Holding anger blinds you to your spouse's gifts and values for your life and keeps you from seeing his or her efforts to make things better.

There's a better way. "Bear with each other and forgive one another if any of you has a grievance against someone. Forgive as the Lord forgave you" (Colossians 3:13). What breaks you out of these anger ruts is the sweet remembrance of the massive debt of ours that our Lord Jesus forgave. If we show a bitter and unforgiving spirit to our spouse, we are daring God to do the same to us.

Certain things to never say to your Spouse

I believe that marriage can be a beautiful thing and certainly to be enjoyed. The truth is that if you find a godly spouse, indeed, you find a good thing. But the reality is that no relationship is perfect and sometimes your spouse will say something that gets on your nerves. To be honest, we've all been there if married long enough.

This ones for husband and wife, there are list of things better left unsaid to your spouse. It's not all inclusive and this isn't to point either of you out. I know that there are some things better left unsaid or comments that might bother either of you that can cause damage to your relationship.

Every woman wants a husband who will care for her and watch over her. She wants a protector and to feel taken care of. I believe that because of this, it's nice when you as the husband notice that your wife might need help with something and this will be the opportunity for you to jump in for the support.

For instance your wife might need assistance reaching for a bowl above the fridge or picking up the plate from the top kitchen cabinet. This is a great opportunity for you as the husband to jump in and serve your wife. If you don't jump in and maybe she seems frustrated or mentions she would have like helped. Refrain from commenting she should have asked for it. A comment like that will leave her feeling alone and uncared for. I promise you, it's the little things that go a long way.

Sometimes the logic is, if I know we won't agree on the topic or see eye to eye, let's not talk about it. The truth is that, not talking about it doesn't make the difference go away. If anything, it creates a gap that will only grow with time. This often happens in family life, politics and even in the Bible.

Let me encourage you not to be afraid to talk to your wife regarding a sensitive issue just because you don't think you'll agree. Take the opportunity to really listen to each other and grow closer through the differences.

I want you to understand that when husband and wife are working on any project or on something they care about and have pour lots of time into, I believe both husband and wife will look for encouragement and validation from one another. What you mustn't do is start critiquing how your spouse is going about the project.

Avoid making statements that call into question her ability as this will significantly discourage her. It's okay to complement and then ask, "have you ever thought of trying this?" This approach encourages her and leads to bettering each other, rather than critiquing.

Let's look at this scenarios such as your wife gets a new haircut or works out to lose a few pounds or tries out a new makeup look. She wants to know you notice and might ask "how do I look" or "can you tell I made a change?" If so, never say anything close to "you look the same to me"

Your wife wants you to notice her, in both the small and significant ways. Make a comment about how you like the new look or appreciate the hard work she's put into the new effort. This is one of many secrets for the husband and wife to have a successful marital life.

Most Difficult Things about Divorce (And What You Can Do to Help Those Going through It).

Divorce is an unfortunate reality in today's church. The church is said to have more divorce rate than ever before. And regardless of which side you stand on the issue, as Christians, we are called to reach out to those in need to show the love of Christ.

And like any issue in the church or society at large, it is best handled when it is understood. With that in mind, consider the difficult things the divorced in your church have been through and what you can do to minister to them.

1. Unfathomable Grief

Going through divorce is an actual tearing of the flesh where two had become one. The tear is painful and slow and a literal death of everything we hoped for, dreamed about, and worked for our entire lives.

Unlike other losses, it's often compounded when lifelong friends avoid you, family walks away from you, and strangers you've never met discuss your personal matters as if they were privy to such things. While other tragedies result in people gathering to help, offer support, and stand with you, the opposite often occurs when a family dissolves through divorce.

What you can do:

Offer condolences just as you would if a death occurred. Offer to bring a meal, or simply sit with the person who's grieving. You will likely be one of very few who do so and it will mean more than you can imagine.

2. The Turning of an Ex

Some go through divorce as adults and are able to put the children first. Unfortunately, that is a very small group. For many, divorce becomes an unexpected battlefield where the person you once trusted with your life becomes the person who will stop at nothing to destroy your efforts to rebuild it.

What you can do:

Check in on them. Too often, these situations can escalate to a dangerous level when others pull away and the person left to deal with it feels alone. Ask questions about how the relationship is going with their ex and encourage them to seek help if you think it is needed. When you are knee-deep in an overwhelming situation, it's often hard to see or accept the gravity of it.

3. How Some Christians Respond

The way some in the church respond to divorce is mind-boggling. While they will offer up ministries to combat causes of divorce (adultery, substance abuse, sexual deviancy, physical abuse), they condemn those who remove themselves from these unbiblical lifestyles.

As a result, many who are divorced or considering it as the only way to protect themselves and their children, will slowly fade from the church at the time they need it the most in their lives. It's hard not to feel shunned by God when so many Christians are so vocal with their opinions about divorce. Just like anyone who's suffered a great loss, the divorced often look at God and question His part in it.

What you can do:

Show them extra grace. Be the one who follows Jesus instead of the crowd and show them what the love of Christ physically looks like without placing judgment on the person who is suffering. For someone who feels reprimanded unfairly, this can be one of the most healing moments in their walk and might pull them toward God instead of away from Him.

4. Our Children's Pain

There's nothing more important to a parent than protecting their children. So please try to understand that the vast majority of parents who choose divorce are doing so because the situation they were living in was causing greater harm to their children than they think the break up of a family will. No one goes into this lightly.

This is especially true for those in the church. Many will stay in unhealthy or dangerous situations for years in order to keep their children with both parents. So understand that anyone who has decided divorce is the only option is still heartbroken at what their actions will do—even if their decision is actually a courageous one that will stop harmful situations and give their children a better future.

What you can do:

Encouraging any single parent you know by noticing the positive things in their new version of family continue to include them just as you did before the family dissolved, no matter how awkward it may be for you momentarily.

There are a million emotions wrapped up in divorce. Sadness, anger, hopelessness, relief, insecurity, bitterness, and all of those (and more) can happen within a single day.

When you are caught in a whirlwind, it's hard to focus on the positive when you are struggling to simply take care of your children at the most basic of levels. Be a good example of God's love, acceptance, and forgiveness. You never know how your small efforts could make a huge difference in a suffering family.

Chapter 10
Bad Reasons To Leave Your Marriage

I know how you feel. You're tired of trying. On some days you feel like you're ready to give up. But before you walk away from what you once hoped would last forever, let me share with you something that might spare you future regret.

After 29 years of marriage and nearly 20 years counselling and coaching other couples who were ready to give up, I've learned that there are certain phrases or "reasons" that one or both spouses will cite for why a marriage is crumbling. Yet these reasons are often ones that one or both parties later realized were workable.

Here are "Bad Reasons for Leaving Your Marriage"

1. **"You don't meet my emotional needs."** You and I might not say it this way, but we sure think it. And the truth is our spouse can never meet our emotional needs. That tank can only be filled by God. If you leave your marriage thinking someone else out there can fulfil you more and give your life meaning and meet your every need, you'll be sorely disappointed again.

2. For many years, I've been taking people to Isaiah 54:5 to reflect on God's words through the prophet Isaiah: *"For your husband is your Maker, Whose name is the Lord of hosts…"* May I let you know that your best bet is to look to God as your spiritual husband to meet your needs for security, fulfilment, communication, a sense of purpose, and so on.

   As you look to God as your primary source of fulfilment, you are freeing up your spouse, emotionally, to do the best he can with a much lighter load. I can't tell you how many people I've shared this with who now wish they had known and practiced this principle of looking to God to be their "spiritual husband" before they left their marriages.

3. **"You've changed through the years."** There's no doubt your spouse has changed through the years. We all have. Just as you may claim your spouse is not the same person today that you married years ago, neither are you. We rarely know the person we are marrying until we live in close quarters with them, experience conflict with them, work through struggles with them, and see them on their worst days.

   You may feel you have outgrown your spouse through the years, or you might simply feel you are with someone you don't know anymore, but if he or she is willing to live with you, in spite of your own changes, give it another chance.

4. **"We don't talk anymore."** I understand this one more than you know. I've been married over 28 years to a woman who does share her feelings, verbally. And being a communicator myself, this means it takes a lot of work to make sure we are emotionally connecting. But as long as one of you is willing to talk, there is hope. If you are the one who initiates the communication, keep initiating.

   When both parties give up trying, that's when the marriage is in trouble. I know many wives (and some husbands, too) who tired after a while of feeling that they were the only ones trying to communicate and keep the relationship moving forward. As far as it depends on you, be the talker. Be the one who tries the hardest.

   The Bible says in (1 Corinthians 13:8), that godly love *"bears all things, believes all things, hopes all things, endures all things"* – even when it comes to the communication that your spouse doesn't seem to be doing.

5. **"We'll both be happier without each other."** Really? We can tell ourselves this when we think in terms of finding someone new to appreciate us more. We can tell ourselves this on the days when things are really bad and we want to be free of those days, altogether.

   But there is a price to be paid with broken promises, divided estates, dashed dreams, and the undoing of a commitment that was, at one time, "till death separates us." And if you and your spouse have children, please don't think for a moment "they will be better off." That is a lie we tell ourselves to justify our breakup and experience our own contentment.

   Unless it is a case of physical, verbal, sexual, or emotional abuse, children (regardless of their ages) are never better off through divorce than if their parents had stayed together. In addition, may I say that your happiness was never a condition for the vows you took.

You promised to love unconditionally "for better or for worse, in sickness and in health" and in the majority of vows I've witnessed there was no clause that said "as long as we both are happy." God's goal for your marriage is to make you and your spouse holy, not happy. And often we don't become holier by getting rid of what doesn't make us happy.

We become holier, and more like Christ, through the situations we endure, not escape. And if your reason is "I've found someone else I'm more compatible with," that new relationship is just as volatile as your existing one because you will be taking your issues, wounds, and unmet expectations to someone else.

I am so grateful that God will never move on to someone else because He has found me and my problems unworkable. We are all broken. Sin has wreaked havoc in our world and relationships. But we can trust the One who *"causes all things to work together for good to those who love God, to those who are called according to His purpose"* (Romans 8:28).

6. **"I need to find myself."** I've talked with many people who married young, had children at a very young age, and then left their marriages, claiming "I didn't know who I was. I had to find my identity." The sad truth was that nearly every one of them found who they were – a divorced, single mom struggling to make ends meet and bitter at the circumstances that life had "brought" them.

   Jesus said in (Matthew 10:39): *He who has found his life will lose it, and he who has lost his life for My sake will find it.* Selfishness says "My life is about me." Godliness says "My life is God's and I will trust Him with where I am right now and how He chooses to work through it."

   Before I start writing this book I have seen marriages that have deteriorated through abandonment, abuse, addiction, sexual unfaithfulness, and betrayal. I know those situations grieve the heart of God and those who are hurt by them. And if that is your case, please get counsel, help, accountability, and much prayer support as you take the necessary steps to be free of that bondage.

I am writing this book particularly for the spouse who is considering one of the above statements as the *primary* reason for leaving the marriage. Think it through carefully. Pray about it. Talk to your pastor or trusted Christian friend who can give you biblical, rather than worldly advice.

Anyone can leave a marriage. It takes a person with integrity, faith, trust in the God of reconciliation, and hope in the God who restores to stick it out through thick and thin. Can *you* be that person?

Chapter 11
Ways To Make Memories With Your Spouse When You've Been Married For A Long Time.

The Bible says, *"But may the righteous be glad and rejoice before God; may they be happy and joyful."* (Psalm 68:3) Hey, guess what? Your marriage can be MORE FUN! You can discover Psalm 68:3 first hand--be glad, rejoice before God, and be happy and joyful—just by hanging out with your spouse. Don't believe it? This week, try these budget-friendly, relationship-building, memory-making exercise and find out for yourself...

1. Guess what's in your spouse's wallet or purse.

Imagine you're a mentalist performing in a big show, then pick your spouse "randomly" out of the audience (or, well, out of the recliner). Take turns, and see if you can each guess up to 10 items that are currently in your spouse's wallet or purse. When you're done, compare your lists to see who got the most guesses right. Then ask what your lists reveal about each of you. Before you're done, swap one item from each list as a souvenir of this experience.

2. Ask questions about the Bible.

May I suggest you try this experiment with your spouse: Read an entire book of the Bible with a notepad right beside you. Each time a question about what you're reading pops into your head, jot it down. (For example, "What exactly is a Leviathan?" "Why should we fear God?" "What does this verse really mean?" and so on.) When you're finished, work together with your spouse to find answers. Check out Bible commentaries, ask leaders at your church, and get insight from friends to search out answers to the questions you wrote. Hey, you just might learn something important together!

3. Create a new dessert to share.

In the olden days, romance was just two straws in a single drugstore-soda. Today our standards are higher. So...grab your spouse and gather your five favourite sweets. Then begin experimenting to find the best way to combine all five items into one super-duper, sharable dessert! For example, you might stick a candy bar into a slice of cheesecake, sprinkle it with jelly beans, crumble carrot cake into fudge sauce, and pour the sauce over the whole concoction. How romantic!

4. Say "I love you" seven different ways.

The goal here is to be able to say "I love you" to your spouse in a different way each day of the week. For instance, on Sunday you might say "Ife mi" which is (of course) "my love" in Yoruba. On Monday, you might etch the words into a steam-covered mirror. On Tuesday, you might leave Hershey's Kisses and a handwritten copy of your favourite Scripture in the kitchen or in the bedroom where she can see it. On Wednesday you could buy your spouse a new perfume or aftershave. (I'm joking.) But you get the idea. Come up with ideas of creative ways to express your undying love for your spouse, and then spend next week trying out each and every one!

5. Mail your spouse a letter.

Take time to write a lovey-romantic sticky-sweet letter to your spouse, knowing it'll be two or three days until he or she gets it. Write what you especially love about your spouse, what you're currently reading in the Bible, your favourite thing from time with your spouse today, one special prayer you are praying for your spouse, and anything you want that person to remember like (I love you" or don't forget to hug me). Go ahead and mail it. See how much changes in the time it takes for your spouse to receive it.

6. Look at the sky.

Want to know something cool? The "night sky" that awed King David in Psalm 8:3-4 is pretty much the same today as it was when he saw it thousands of years ago. So, what are you and your spouse waiting for? If possible (and safe), climb on your roof while you do this. Lie on your backs and take in the show going on above you, day or night. Count the number of colours you see in the sky. See how far you can focus your vision (be careful not to look directly in the sun in the daytime, though!). Pick out the farthest star at night. In daytime, take a moment to ponder that the daylight you feel started 93,000,000 miles away from where you are right now. And if the sun's just right and the wind smells sweet, feel free to take a quick nap and enjoy the day.

A Spouse's Prayer.

Dear Jesus, thank you so much for giving me a spouse with whom I can be glad, rejoice before You, and be happy and joyful (Psalm 68:3). Thank you for giving me a reason to rejoice always with my spouse, to pray continually for my spouse and my marriage, and to give thanks in all circumstances in my marriage knowing this is God's will for me in Christ Jesus (1 Thessalonians 5:16–18). You are the awesome God, and I see that in the blessing of my spouse. I'm so grateful in Jesus name. Amen!

Chapter 12
The One Thing You Must Have If You Want Good Communication With Your Spouse... No Exceptions.

onesty is one thing that needs to be present before you can even begin having or improving communication with your spouse. And not only do you have to be honest, but you also have to be honest often. Do just one or the other, or none at all, and you risk constructing your communication on shaky ground. This is what I mean.

Honesty is a must!

Honesty is very bottom rung on the communications ladder; it is the basis for all communication with your spouse. If you aren't communicating honestly, you would be better off communicating nothing at all. The message you send provides the basis for the feedback you'll get. If the original message is untrue, how can the feedback be of any value to the relationship?

The whole truth is that if you aren't communicating honestly, you would be better off communicating nothing at all. This doesn't just apply to dishonesty with the intention to deceive; this applies to openly communicating your thoughts, desires, and needs.

For instance, on one Sunday afternoon, when my family was having one of those dinners where everyone was doing their own thing. The oldest of my 3 sons is already sitting at the table eating his food and at the same time playing game on his laptop with the headphones on.

I sat at the table, not eating, just waiting for my wife to bring the rest of the food to the table. All of a sudden, I realised that he is still playing his game while eating. Then I asked him, "What are you doing?" He replied, "Just playing games dad! Do you want me to stop playing the game?"

Then I replied, "No. I'm just asking," To be honest, I fully expecting him to stop playing the game and take off the headphones so that he can concentrate on his food. But, he didn't. He kept on playing his game while I sat at the table in silence annoyed that he was being rude. Then I realized that he had given me exactly what I asked for. Which is not what I wanted. I didn't ask for what I wanted because I didn't feel like I should have to ask for something that *in my mind* should be obvious.

So I instead decided to be dishonest about communicating what I wanted. My message was untrue, and his feedback in response to my false message only left me angry at the end. If you are honest about communicating your needs, you give your partner the option to be receptive to those needs. If you continue to ask for things you don't want, you'll probably keep getting them.

Now let's be honest about honesty.

It's not always easy to say what you mean. Sometimes it's because you don't want to hurt your spouse's feelings. Other times it's because you don't want to deal with a negative consequence to an action or opinion. So how do you facilitate honesty in your relationship even when honesty is hard? Let me encourage you with few tips:

Minimise your blow-ups.

If your spouse thinks every time he comes to you with honesty he'll experience one of your meltdowns, honesty in your relationship becomes a scary thing. Every reaction won't be positive, but try to keep calm enough so that your spouse won't be afraid of coming to you again. Starting with a simple, "I appreciate your honesty..." can start positive communication off on the right foot.

Own up to the consequences of your actions.

None of us are perfect. We all make mistakes. But part of being an adult is recognizing those mistakes and owning up to them, even if we face an undesirable consequence. Remember that as angry or hurt as your spouse may be with the truth, she will be even more hurt when she finds out that she's been the victim of a lie.

Being dishonest is not only childish, it's selfish. By not telling the truth you are telling your spouse, "I would rather hurt you and our marriage with a lie than face the consequences of my own actions." Know that when you are dishonest, you are protecting yourself at the expense of your marriage.

Be honest in your behaviour.

Remember that "behaviour" part of communication we talked about earlier? What you do communicates just as much, if not more, to your spouse than what you say. Following through on what you say you will do and staying away from activities that you know make you look untrustworthy communicates to your spouse that you are dependable and worthy of trust without you having to say a word.

How to keep the communication doors open

In addition to making sure your communication is honest, you also need to make sure you are exchanging intentional messages on a regular basis. We are communicating with our spouses constantly without thinking about it. Any time you are interacting with one another, you're communicating back and forth, but you aren't always communicating on purpose.

Think about your place of employment. If your company is run well, likely there is regular communication between the employer and the employees. Sometimes it is informal, like asking a colleague for help on a project you don't understand or sending an email to a coworker to ask for something you need to finish a project.

Sometimes it's formal, like annual reviews or weekly staff meetings. Either way, you are transmitting and receiving information regularly throughout your day to stay on top of your job and to keep your place of employment running smoothly.

The same is true of marriage. You have to communicate frequently and on purpose to your spouse to ensure that life is running smoothly at home, and you have to have a regular system of doing it alongside the informal methods you use. Finally, here are a few ways to keep the communication doors open in a positive way on a regular basis such as to:

Give compliments every day.

It is a good habit for husband and wife to give compliments to each other every day. You want to make sure that your positive communication outweighs the negative. Often we think of communicating only when we have an issue. But communication is at the basis of all of your interactions.

If you can speak positivity and communicate to your spouse that he or she is loved and appreciated, when you *do* have to communicate about a conflict it won't seem like all of your communication and feedback has a negative spin. It places optimism at the front of the communications cycle to make that flow of communication more positive each time.

Create quality time to spend with one another

Again, this goes back to behaviour as communication. By making your spouse's time a priority, you communicate that he or she is important enough to forego other life aspects in that moment, and takes precedence over the rest of your to-do list. In addition, unless you spend all of your time together staring at the wall in silence, it becomes natural to communicate during the quality time you spend.

Set up a regularly occurring time that you sit down together to discuss the larger issues

Some larger issues could be finances, health, household, and goal setting. This could be weekly or monthly, but making time to get on the same page with one another on a regular basis is essential. Don't let areas of conflict linger.

Chapter 13
Ways To Improve Your Marriage.

Small actions carry surprising power in building a lasting marital life.

I 'll never forget a conversation I had with a couple. She said, "He worked so hard for a year to take us on that amazing vacation to America. But all I really wanted was for him to put his arm around me at church!"

I could fill in lots of other details, but ultimately the pattern is a sadly common one. You may have seen it too. Paul was a godly, well-intentioned husband who showed his love in several ways, including working long hours to provide for his family and to do nice things for them. You see, for him, providing is love.

Unfortunately, he didn't realize that what he was working so hard for wasn't what Angela most needed, and in some ways was actually robbing her of the closeness she needed the most. (And of course there were ways she didn't know she was hurting him.) What she needed most, more than all the expensive vacations in the world, were a few simple, specific day-to-day actions.

But as simple as loving gestures in public? **you wonder.**

Yes! with my experience in marriage counselling and in my marriage, I realised that many happy couples do an extraordinarily work on their marriage (often without realizing it!) doing a few little specific actions that were making their spouses feel deeply cared for. Angela, as it turns out, is like nearly all other men and women in her deep rooted desire for these surprisingly meaningful gestures.

Day-to-day actions

Clearly, a few small actions won't fix deep relationship problems. But for most of us, a handful of simple day-to-day actions increase *the likelihood that our spouse feels that we care deeply about them, instead of feeling that we don't.* I believe that there's just enormous power in that!

The truth is that for nearly every man or woman, the same few small, gender-specific actions not only matter but have a huge impact on a couple's level of happiness. But these little actions take on even more power when accompanied by those that matter to your spouse individually.

In other word, *you are* very likely to make your spouse feel deeply cared for, if you make a habit of doing a little more things consistently. For instance, a wife will have a big impact on the husband's happiness when she notices his effort and sincerely thanks him for it.

For example, the wife may say to the husband "Thank you for mowing the lawn even though it was so hot outside." Or, "Thanks for playing with the kids, even when you were so tired from work. This deeply will please any husband at any time. *Another instance what the wife* might say is "You did a great job at your friend birthday party last night." This will deeply please many husband too.

It is a good and encouraging habit for a wife to appreciate the husband in front of others something he did well. That will boost a man ego and make him to become better in what he does and a good husband generally.

Another area I would not shy away from to mention that is very important in marriage is the area of sex between husband and wife. Let me encourage every wives to desires his husband sexually most of the time and every husband to pleases the wife sexually all the time. It will help your marriage to stand the test of time.

This is one of the ways that a wife makes it clear to the husband that he makes her happy. (For example, she expresses appreciation for something he did for her with a smile, words, a big hug, etc.) This will make any husband too happy because when your wife is happy, you too are happy.

May I encourage you the husband to start practising the habit that will have a big impact on your wife that will improve your marriage. For instance, takes your wife hand when walking through a parking lot or sitting together at the movies. I know that this will deeply pleases all women.

This is one of the things I do every day to connect with my wife even though we may not be in the same physical location. I leave her a message by voice mail, text or WhatsApp during the day to say that I love her and thinking about her. This deeply will please most of the women.

It is a good practise to puts your arm around your wife or lays your hand on your wife knee when you are sitting next to each other in public (at church, at a restaurant with friends, etc.). This is to say to your wife that you are still in love with her no matter the situation and I know this will deeply pleases all women.

Let me encourage every husbands to complement your wife frequently by telling her sincerely that "You are beautiful." Such accolade will make your wife to believe in herself as a beautiful woman and she will always make sure to look radiant for you most of the time.

As you may notice that *all* these happiness-inducing actions are simple, learnable, and doable by any wife or any husband? If you put each of the examples to work every day, I believe without a shadow of doubt, your marriage will improve, in most cases, radically. I know that you want your marriage to improve and that is why you are reading this book.

The truth is that all these small but powerful actions matter regardless of what the person's love language is. For example, most wives are affected when her husband reaches out and takes her hand, regardless of whether physical touch is her thing.

I'm so thankful that God is good. He is always at work to redeem our broken hearts and I know He'll do it for you too. We all know that small, thoughtful acts are not a magic cure, all for every marriage problem. With simple but powerful actions, I believe that you and I can build that all important foundation that will helps us believe that our mate notices and cares.

I want you to know that, *believing that the other person cares* is far more important to building a happy marriage than most of us ever realized **because it is one of the secrets for a successful marriage.**

Husband and Wife Responsibility to make their Marriage work.

Given my experience, there are some key concepts I learned in my journey as well. Both husband and wife have equal responsibility in making their marriage work. For all the points mentioned for husbands in this chapter are perhaps also for wives that will help your marriage successful.

Let me encourage every wife to always seek out the best for her husband. Dwell on those things, not what you don't like about him.

Every loving, responsible and committed wife need to have sex with her own husband often and most of the time if need be. I got this advice from a marriage journal, from an older married woman writer many years ago: Make love a lot, especially when you don't feel like it. Making love is a balm, it covers and heals a lot of the wounds we inflict on one another in a marriage. When you feel like you just aren't close to your spouse, that's the time to take off your clothes and get close.

Seek counsel from older, wiser women who have succeeded in their marriages. It's impossible to make good decisions when we're emotional. And seeking counsel from your friends who are your own age isn't as good as counsel from elderly women. Let your husband zone out. He is not ignoring you, men just have moments of brain freeze. It's not your job to change or fix your him. Both of you are on a journey. Tell your husband how big/strong/smart/manly he is all the time. They tend to forget. Never forget or take for granted that your man chose you.

Laugh at his jokes. Even if they aren't funny. We are responsible for our reactions, no one else. We must take full accountability of our emotions and how we respond. And so must he. Make him that food he likes as often as time permits. Allow your man to just be. Be a comfort, be a gentle and giving spirit when the times call for it.

Quit being nasty when he gets home, let him chill. Love him in the way he needs it, not the way you assume he needs it. Find out your different love languages and be sensitive and ready to show him you love him in ways he understands best.

Make yourself look pretty as much as you can especially if you have married for a long time. The more feminine you act the more it reminds him he is a man. Be present and give him your time and attention when he needs it. In my experience, during those times I did serve my wife, she over time, served me and now it is vice versa.

May I advice you on this, to never talk about other men, even if they are fictional or movie, even if it's to say "you are so much hotter than that guy" Most men already think they are, so this will confuse them. Be willing to have him sexually. Let him know you need his masculine presence, that you trust him fully.

Never read advice on the internet from strangers. They probably don't know you and will make you do stupid things that will not be applicable or appropriate in your marriage…Give him space. He needs times to find his new self (we change constantly) before he can give of himself.

By doing these things it would not mean a wife doesn't expect her husband to be great too or is to blame for the breakdown, just that she is doing her part to make a better half of a marriage. Be vulnerable and do not be afraid to share your fears and feelings. Men tend to know when you are keeping things from them. And they know when their wife is transparent. And, I can't emphasize this more: acknowledge your mistakes. Say you're sorry when you know you need to.

Allow your husband to love you his way instead of comparing his expression of love to your own ideals. If you keep comparing, you may miss the most beautiful moments of tenderness. Do not be afraid to be fully transparent. This builds great trust over time.

Don't ever, ever, ever put your spouse down in public! He has to have someone that he knows will have his back. If you need to discuss something he did or said, do it in private. No one wants to be corrected in front of others. Once discussed and fixed, let it go!

Find common hobbies, goals, and dreams. Also, find common ground in your faith. Never stop growing together. Laugh lots. Fall in love over and over again. Many times, a wife cannot connect or reconnect because she

Chapter 14
Ways To Divorce-Proof Your Marriage.

In the beginning, God created a marriage. Not a government. Not a school. Not a committee. (A marriage). This intimate relationship is the foundation on which God chose to build every human relationships. God performed the first marriage, and from one marriage came the world's inhabitants. But as with all the holy and precious things God creates, the enemy is quick to level crushing attacks against it, and your marriage is no different.

Even if your marriage is near perfect, it's important that you go out of your way to protect this most sacred of relationships, which is only second to your relationship with God Himself. The Bible says, "Stay alert! Watch out for your great enemy, the devil. He prowls around like a roaring lion, looking for someone to devour." (1Peter 5:8).

Indeed, the enemy relishes any opportunity to devour marriage, as it is the foundation of all human relationships. So, how can you "stay alert" in regard to your marriage at this time when anything goes to attack marriages?

Here are some practical truths that can help divorce-proof your marriage.

Remove Divorce From Your Language

The Bible says "Avoid worthless, foolish talk that only leads to more godless behaviour." (2 Timothy 2:16). This is what the Bible say, "The tongue can bring death or life; those who love to talk will reap the consequences." (Proverbs 18:21).

The Scriptures reminds us constantly that our words hold great power, and just like with anything else, the power of life or death for your marriage is in your tongue. Don't even joke about divorce, don't use it as a threat, and certainly don't entertain divorce as a "Plan B" or an escape route.

While it may seem inconsequential, when you speak words about the death of your marriage, which is divorce, you give the 'divorce weed' a chance to take root in your marriage. Rip it from your vocabulary like you would a weed growing in your garden.

Remember That Marriage Is Not Intended to Complete You.

Hear this, "On the last day, the climax of the festival, Jesus stood and shouted to the crowds, 'Anyone who is thirsty may come to me! Anyone who believes in me may come and drink! For the Scriptures declare, "'Rivers of living water will flow from his heart.'" (John 7:37-39).

Many couples constantly expect their marriage relationship to make them whole and they put undue burden and unrealistic expectations on their partner. Truth be told, only God can fully completes and satisfies us. Take a step back and examine your desires and expectations for your spouse.

Let me be real with you and ask this question! Are you expecting your spouse to fulfil a role that only God can fill? If so, it's time to adjust those expectations to line up with God's Word. Begin by looking to God, and only Him, to fill the dry and parched places of your heart with the Living Water of His Spirit.

Believe the Best About Each Other

"She bears up under everything; believes the best in all; there is no limit to her hope, and never will she fall." (1 Corinthians 13:7).

Many marriage battles are fought in the mind before they ever manifest in tangible words and actions. Errant thoughts shoot into the mind like flaming arrows, and if they aren't dealt with immediately, they can cause mass destruction. Thoughts like, *Did he really just say that? Doesn't he know how much that irritates me? That's just like her to do that. A guy can't catch a break.*

Sound familiar? In most circumstances, your spouse isn't out to "get you." Always assuming the worst about your spouse over a misunderstanding is a tiring way to live, and the Bible tells us in (1 Corinthians 13:7) that love "believes the best in all."

If you married your spouse in good conscience that this was indeed who God had for you, why would you assume the worst about him or her? Your spouse, just like you, isn't always going to be perfect, a fact that isn't going to change this side of heaven.

Our lives follow our words (and thoughts!), so what if our first reaction over a misunderstanding with our spouse is to tell ourselves, "Well, this wasn't what I was expecting to happen, but I trust my spouse heart toward me"? How might our relationships improve?

Further communication and resolution may still need to happen, but how much healthier will our attitudes be toward our spouses? And how much more prepared will we be the next time the enemy launches an attack against us if we always believe the best?

Tackle Tough Conversations

The Bible says, *"The mouth of the righteous speaks wisdom, and his tongue talks of justice."* (Psalm 37:30).

Similarly, *"As iron sharpens iron, so a friend sharpens a friend."* (Proverbs 27:17).

While it is important to believe the best about each other, tough topics like purity, children, money, failures and weaknesses can't be avoided. To be an adult is to have the courage and grace to hold those tough conversations. But here's the benefit: Small conversations in the present build bridges for future problem-solving.

Such talks build trust, encourage openness and strengthen the bonds between husband and wife. If you and your spouse rarely circle back to these topics, or if you never even had the conversations to begin with, then it will be much tougher to address them when problems do arise.

Pray for Each Other

I know it is not easy to do because your spouse may use it against you in the near future, but you have to do what the Bible say an let the devil be ashamed "Confess to one another therefore your faults (your slips, your false steps, your offenses, your sins) and pray [also] for one another, that you may be healed and restored [to a spiritual tone of mind and heart].

The earnest (heartfelt, continued) prayer of a righteous man makes tremendous power available [dynamic in its working]." (James 5:16). Building a solid prayer life has its challenges. But there is one person you should remember to pray for every day—your spouse.

Shower your spouse in prayer. Prayer accomplishes exponentially more than you can see or imagine. Prayer has the power to align your will with God's, to change your attitude toward your spouse, and to defend against the enemy's attacks.

Whether in a calm season or a stormy season, set a hedge of prayer around your marriage. "Every time I think of you, I give thanks to my God" (Philippians 1:3).

Set Appropriate Boundaries

May I encourage you today according to what the Bible say to, *"Give honour to marriage, and remain faithful to one another in marriage. God will surely judge people who are immoral and those who commit adultery."* (Hebrews 13:4).

Did you think that boundaries are only for dating couples? Think again! Whether it's technology, money, time or friends, every couple has areas that threaten to weaken the marriage. Because of the time invested in holding those tough conversations, you should know which areas are struggles for you and your spouse.

Own up to those areas, and place some life-giving boundaries in your marriage. Boundaries used in the right way don't restrict life, but open it up for more love and freedom.

Put these steps in place to help you stay alert to the attacks of the enemy, and you're on your way to divorce-proofing your marriage. A marriage takes constant care to carry it through all of the seasons of life.

If you find yourself in a joyous season in your marriage, may this encouragement further strengthen and deepen your roots. But if you find yourself walking through a dark season, do not give up! With God anything is possible! Surround yourself with the Word of God, with prayer and with those who will stand in faith with you. Your marriage is worth it!

Two is better than One in Marriage

We made covenant with one another and we have to be committed to it by God's grace, with understanding and wisdom. According to the books of (Proverb 31). Furthermore the Bible says,

"A wise woman builds her home, but a foolish woman tears it down with her own hands." (Proverb 14:1).

For more understanding, the Scriptures emphasised that *"But there is one thing I want you to know: The head of every woman is man, and the head of Christ is God." (1 Corinthians 11:3).* In another verse of the Bible, it says, *"For a husband is the head of his wife as Christ is the head of the church. He is the Saviour of his body, the church." (Ephesian 5:23-24).*

The Bible makes it clear in, "Titus 2:2-8). These are the original role of a married woman and the man. The divine principles and the older ones should be an inspiration to younger generations more so, it is our test often faith.

Marriage is the only institution that God ordained and it is a blessings and favour. Marriage is our training ground. The man is the head, Priest, King and a Leader. Woman cannot contest or compete with them. Men are not perfect and women are not perfect either.

We have gone through a lots together and we are still standing, it is about the Will of God not our own will or emotion. How we feel or how it should be or what people said or our thought however, no condition is permanent, we are all learning and growing everyday.

We just need to learn how to appreciate our differences, strengths and weaknesses and give ourselves time, space and focus. Divorce and living single or separating from one another is not the best solution. A virtuous woman built her home with God's wisdom.

The fear of God is the beginning of wisdom. It is about relationship with God and obeying His laws/commandments that matters. Love one another, It is about patience, understanding and endurance, it is about tolerance and not with provocation, arrogance, pride, competition, violence, pretence, deceit nor suffering silent but by prayers and seeking for help when needed.

We all need one another as the Lord stated that it is not good for man to leave alone .....the male is for strength while the female is for comfort. May the only wise God answers all your prayers. May his grace and wisdom keep us together in Jesus name. Amen.

Chapter 15
Blue Print Of A Healthy Marriage.

Oladunni and I celebrated our 29th Wedding Anniversary this year 2019. We thank God for His grace upon our family. I want you to know that one of the fun things about your anniversary is to look back, not only on your wedding day, but also on the grace God has shown you throughout your entire marriage. In particular you can look over the entirety of your marriage and see how the Lord has been at work in you.

Truth be told, I thought I knew a lot about marriage when we got married twenty eight years ago because I had memorized Ephesians 5 and read some books, but the following months and years proved I didn't know much at all. God is good though, and in His faithfulness He has helped us both to grow, mature, and experience a portion of the joy the Lord intended marriage to be when he ordained it in the garden.

The Lord has been teaching me through our marriage, through His word, through talking with other Christians, and by His Spirit over the last twenty eight years. May I share with your four blue prints that seem to be present in healthy and growing marriages.

1. Permanence.

Anyone can get excited to work on their marriage for a few minutes, but growing marriages require daily work. Somebody said, likens marriage to a garden. You cannot plant a garden, ignore it, and expect to see fruit. Instead, you must do the hard work of pulling weeds and cultivating crops. In the same way, marriages require consistent effort over the long haul.

We work on our marriages by cultivating kindness, forgiveness, time together, listening, and a host of other virtues. We must also weed out anger, bitterness, selfishness, rudeness, wandering eyes, and any other sin that effects your marriages.

If you inspect the garden every day to look for growth, you probably don't see perceptible movement, but over the course of weeks you begin to see fruit. In the same way, we only see growth in our marriage over the course of time and this growth only takes place when spouses are committed to each other for the rest of their lives.

Marriages grow because spouses are growing, and many people will not take the time to make the difficult changes that need to be made when they are not committed for the rest of their lives. Marriage requires serious self-reflection, repentance, compassion, forgiveness, and self-forgetfulness.

These virtues don't form in our hearts overnight and it does not happen without painful changes. When you are in your marriage for the rest of your life, you will commit to making the changes you need to make because I believe that you value the glory of God and your spouse's joy.

2. Teamwork

When I was in secondary school we played all summer season. Many times two boys from the same team would fight each other for a free kick or penalty kick and eventually someone would shout, "same team." These two guys struggled against each other when they should be working together and had to be reminded they were on the same side.

We need this same reminder in marriage sometimes. Spouses take out their bad days on each other, snap at each other when the children have been misbehaving, or work against each other instead of working together. In this situation the only answer is for spouses to stop and remember that they are in this together. We have to remember we have the same ultimate goals for lasting joy and the glory of God followed by a commitment to stop acting as if our spouse is a problem and remember they are our partner.

Many of the obstacles married couples face will be reduced in size when we face them as one. This doesn't mean they go away, but we go into difficulties with a completely different mind-set when we know we are together. Going in to face problems at work, sickness, overwhelming bills, and disobedient children as a united couple give couples support and comfort they don't have when they are divided.

3. Thoughtfulness

So often when we have problems in our marriages, we don't need a seminar to help us because our greatest struggles come from treating each other in an ungodly way. We speak rashly, hold grudges, forget how to show patience and empathy, and speak to each other in ways we would never tolerate if the shoe was on the other foot. Couples work against each other, undermine each other, and forget to show each other even the most basic courtesy.

Many times, the answer is to apply "love your neighbour as yourself" and the "one another" passages to our marriages. After all, isn't our spouse our closest neighbour? How much would our marriages change if we obeyed "bearing with one another and forgiving one another, as the Lord has forgiven you, so also should you?"

What kind of practical difference would it be, if you show basic kindness and only treat your spouse the way you want to be treated? We overcomplicate marriage, and think we need some kind of specialized training when we really just need to show love, kindness, patience, and forgiveness. I can tell you that this one change makes overwhelming difference.

4. Friendship

About fifteen to twenty years ago everyone started talking about the importance of date night for marital health. Especially when couples have small children, getting away for a few hours is an important ingredient in your marriage. We can have fun and enjoy our time together, especially since we don't have other people to feed instead of ourselves.

However, it is the couple's only quality time together which is a date night, but we are missing some of the best opportunities for our marriage to grow. Nothing helps our marriage grow like daily time together. Working on projects together, cooking and cleaning the kitchen together, and hanging out together after the kids gone to bed are some of the best times we can have together.

This kind of time together over time builds friendship, helps us work out problems together, and gives moments of joy in the midst of tough days.

The time we need together everyday must be intentionally carved out. No one ever magically "finds time" for important things because if something is truly important we must make time for it.

This means aligning schedules and cutting out extra activities if necessary. It involves getting kids in bed or in their rooms at a decent hour or getting up before the kids wake up to have breakfast together. Whatever form it may take, repeated quality time builds a truly loving and lasting friendship.

We don't talk enough about the role of friendship in marriage. We think of friends as the people who live outside of our own homes, but if we are in union together shouldn't our spouses be our closest friends? Shouldn't this be the person I want to spend time with the most and be more willing to confide in than anyone else?

If it is not the case, if we want to run from our spouses instead of spend time with them, it serves as a reminder for us to walk in repentance and forgiveness towards them. If years of anger and hostility have driven a barrier between spouses, the answer is to repent, forgive, and reconcile with them so the barrier is torn down and the friendship restored.

Things That Make for a Healthy Marriage

Every marriage contains its share of challenges. There will be difficult seasons in even the happiest of unions. It might be an overstatement to compare marriage to a rollercoaster, but even a healthy relationship is like a country road, with its twists and turns and occasional dips. The key is how you respond to the challenges.

Let me encourage every Christian men and women that is able to read this book to examine their own lives and behaviour. Marriage is not an entitlement. It's a gift that too many of us have squandered. Too many couples, especially Christian couples expect perfection. If you're going through a rough patch, is it possible you're making a mountain out of a molehill?

In this chapter of this book, may I share with you some of the secrets of a healthy marriage that is easy to practice but many couples ignored?

1. High levels of friendship, respect, affection, and humour.

This is defined as liking each other, being each other's best friend, doing things together; showing interest in and respect for the other's thoughts and feelings, avoiding put-downs, supporting each other's goals and aspirations, feeling affection for each other, having fun and laughter together, being number one in each other's eyes.

2. A ratio of 5:1 or better of positive to negative interactions.

This means that your relationship averages at least five pleasant, friendly, or loving experiences or periods of time for every hostile word, angry argument, or time spent feeling hurt or resentful. And 5:1 is the minimum!

3. Successful "bids for attention"

When a wife says, "Hey, listen to this!" she is trying to get her husband's attention for a conversation. If the husband keeps on scrolling through Facebook, ignoring her, he's turning away her bid for attention. If he says "Huh?" and lifts his eyes off the sports page for a second or two, he's turning toward her—a good sign. And if he actually listens to what she has to say, that's a real connection! In successful marriages, partners turn toward each other an average of 86 percent of the time. In divorcing couple's, the average is 33 percent.

4. Soft starts of disagreements.

In successful marriages, disagreements are started softly, without critical, contemptuous remarks about the other person.

5. Husbands accepts influence from wife.

In successful marriages, husbands accept influence from their wives. If a wife says she's afraid her husband is driving too fast and he responds in irritation, "I know what I'm doing!" this is a shaky marriage. There must be give and take in a relationship. Research shows that women are accustomed to accepting influence from men. So it's crucial that men learn to do the same!

6. Respect for each other's needs, likes, dislikes, and inner life.

They ask questions to find out; they listen; they care!

How did you fare? I pray that you sense the urgency in my words when I remind you that next to your relationship with the Lord, the best investment you can make here on earth is the relationship with your spouse. So much hinges on the health of our marriage.

Yes, marriage is difficult. But remember, it's not designed to make us happy (though it ultimately will); it's designed to make us holy. Somebody said, "If love were only a feeling, there would be no basis for the promise to love each other forever." In other words, the wedding vow anticipates the reality of radical difficulty. It's there in the fine print.

Chapter 16
Marriage Myths

I'll never forget the thrill of being a newlywed – the ecstasy, stunning new realities, and fulfilment that was beyond expectation and description. But I quickly learned that this stage of marriage is short lived. Sooner or later, the valley will come. I've been there.

Some couples are not so fortunate. Many of us have bought into the lie that the goal of marriage is to avoid divorce, but really, it is so much more. The goal is to be happy and to have a good marriage that ultimately glorifies the Lord.

As I reflect on my own marriage, I realized that while there were many factors that played a part in my wife and my ambitions, one of the biggest was my own expectation of what marriage was going to be. I've heard similar sentiments as I have spoken to many couples and with individuals who are hurting and struggling.

In order to realistically approach wedded bliss and live out our calling as man and wife in a biblical marriage, we must recognize common myths that are affecting marriages.

1. Myth:

Because I'm in a Christian marriage,
I'm going to have a perfect marriage.

Truth:

Just because you know Christ doesn't mean there won't be attacks from the enemy against you. Paul reminds us numerous times in his Epistles that even as Christians we will face hardships. The Bible tells us that, "the thief comes only to steal and kill and destroy. I came that they may have life and have it abundantly." (John 10:10). Only with God can you have a strong, healthy marriage.

You can't do it on your own and if you think you can, you are misled. You don't have within you the capabilities, but if you stay committed to God, you will develop the mentality that you're going to stick to this no matter what.

2. Myth:

Certain behaviours or faults can be changed
once marriage takes place.

Truth:

People cannot "create" a spouse. It's important to marry someone for who they are, not what you think you can turn them into. The Bible states: "Do not be usually yoked with unbelievers. For what partnership has righteousness with lawlessness? Or what fellowship has light with darkness?" (2 Corinthians 6:14).

Teams that accomplish great things are those who are unified in their purpose and goals. This is true for marriages, too. If your spouse doesn't follow Christ now it is likely they won't in the future.

3. Myth:

The person I'm marrying is a "knight in shining armour" or "perfect."

Truth:

No one is perfect. Even the godliest people are flawed and stricken by sin leaving them unable to live up to impossible standards. Remember what the Bible say that "all have sinned and fall short of the glory of God." (Romans 3:23).

Marriage is about two people learning to complement the strengths and weaknesses of the other. You must learn to accept your spouse for who they are – flaws and all – just as they must learn to accept you.

4. Myth:

There is always an easy out if it doesn't work.

Truth:

Divorce is never easy and leaves tremendous damage in its wake. God's plan for marriage is forever.

The Bible says that "Jesus answered, "Have you not read that he who created them from the beginning made them male and female, and said, 'Therefore a man shall leave his father and his mother and hold fast to his wife, and the two shall become one flesh. So they are no longer two but one flesh. What God has joined together, let not man separate." (Matthew 19:4-6).

Authentic love never gives in or up. It is without end. God promises that while people will fail authentic love will not. He designed it so it would have in its DNA an unbreakable quality that makes it unstoppable. So many marriages have marginal love, which is based on performance instead of persistence. Ask God to give you the kind of love that endures, sustains, forgives, finds good, is tolerant and constantly looks forward not backward.

5. Myth:

Marriage will be continual sexual ecstasy.

Truth:

This is a big one for most men. Physical intimacy is God's plan but responsibilities, ailments and daily life can bring seasons of lack. Contrary to popular belief, satisfaction and completion are not based on sexual fulfilment. Relationships built on this myth are destined to crumble as couples grow older and physical beauty fades.

Attraction is necessary in a relationship, but true attraction can be found beyond physical beauty. Genuine love is based not on what you can gain from someone but what you can give. Base on (1 Corinthians 13), we are reminded of a long list of things love is and sexual fulfilment is not one of them. Lasting relationships are built on giving without the expectation of receiving in return.

6. Myth:

My spouse will be a romantic Casanova.

Truth:

This tends to trip up many women because it is based on fairy tales. More important than romance is that a spouse loves, cherishes and works to provide emotional and spiritual support. God's intention is for a man to live with his wife with understanding according to his Word, not according to a Hollywood illusion or romantic book facade. If you want a real picture of what this looks like, read (Ephesians 5:22-33).

Even in recognizing these myths, you must also acknowledge there will be ongoing difficulties and challenges in your marriage. However, if you and your spouse continually strengthen communication and commit to working through issues not around them while seeking God's power and protection, you'll grow stronger and have staying power – together.

May I encourage every husband that your *wife wants you to understand that although she may be strong, assertive, secure, and spiritually growing, she still needs you to actively lead her to the cross. It's a no-brainer that men and women process and express themselves differently when it comes to spiritual matters, but your wife needs you to step up to the plate and serve as her spiritual warrior!*

Myths about Sex You Hear in Church.

It's not just the teenagers who propagate myths about sex. We adults are guilty too. Sure, some falsehoods are easy to spot, the sort of ideas that make you shake your head and wonder who would believe that. But other times, we hear, read, and absorb messages about sexuality that simply aren't true.

Unfortunately, some of those myths even come from within our churches or in circles of Christian family and friends. While not always taught directly, these messages seep into our common culture and set up a poor theology about God's design for sex. What myths have been we been floating around? How are they messing up our sexuality? How do they negatively affect our view of God, the creator of sex, and our marriage beds?

Sex is private, so we shouldn't talk about it.

I've heard this one plenty, but here's the problem: God talked about sex. Once old friend of mine decided to read the Bible aloud to his young children, and he quickly found himself wanting to skip over some sections. Because you cannot get very far in the Bible before coming across Scriptures about husbands and wives making love and having children, stories of sexual desire and misconduct, warnings against sinful sexual practices, and poetic passages about sexual intimacy in marriage.

He said, we're only in Genesis chapter two of the Bible, before we get to this gem: *"This explains why a man leaves his father and mother and is joined to his wife, and the two are united into one."* (Genesis 2:24). "United into one" includes physical consummation, or sex.

Now of course we shouldn't know specifics about others' sex lives. But we can discuss God's teaching and principles and give Christians biblically based advice on how to handle challenges in the marriage bed. We can talk about godly sexuality without invading bedroom privacy. Indeed, if we intend to speak where God speaks, we must step up and share God's design for sex.

This was a common belief in the Church for centuries. However, the allegory theory is an outgrowth of Gnosticism, a movement denounced in the New Testament and by early Church leaders. It hung in many respects because of a misunderstanding about the physical versus the spiritual, and frankly some people's discomfort about an erotic book being in the Bible.

With better resources and more study, scholars now believe Song of Songs addresses marital, sexual love. Yes, the Bible does periodically make comparisons between a husband and a wife and God and His people see (Isaiah 54:5 and Ephesians 5:31-32) but this particular book addresses the intimacy of a married couple.

The inclusion of Song of Songs in the Bible demonstrates that God delights in married couples enjoying physical intimacy to the fullest. *"Oh, lover and beloved, eat and drink! Yes, drink deeply of your love!" (Song of Songs 5:1).*

Sex is for procreation.

Well, yes, it is for procreation. Indeed, God's first blessing to humans included His command to *"be fruitful and multiply"* (Genesis 1:28). But the Bible also instructs that we are to make love throughout our marriage, outside of conception. As the Bible says to a man about his wife that, *"She is a loving deer, a graceful doe. Let her breasts satisfy you always. May you always be captivated by her love." (Proverbs 5:19).*

Always means even beyond those times when conception is possible.

Also, in Song of Songs, not once do husband or wife mention conceiving children. Rather, it's clear that they enjoy sex for how it expresses and nurtures mutual love. It helps them to be united into one according to (Genesis 2:24).

When good Christians get married, sex falls into place.

Many couples have been advice during their premarital counselling that: "Sex? You'll work that out when you get married" or, "Sex is pretty straightforward." It's unfortunate that too many pastors and counsellors overlooked an opportunity to share God's design for sexual intimacy in marriage and to leave the door open in case a couple needs to return for assistance.

The truth is that sex can be a struggle for many married couples. Among the potential issues are physical challenges, emotional baggage, difficulty switching from purity to passion, or a mismatch in libidos. Just being Christian doesn't mean that everything will work swimmingly.

What you need to understand is that being a Christian means that God has answers and His community of believers should be there to help. We must reach out to struggling couples in compassionate, concrete ways to help them find godly answers and to embrace healthy, holy intimacy.

Sex is for him.

This is a prevalent myth! Since men are viewed as the ones with a high sex drive, the emphasis gets put on taking care of his desire for sex. Many well-meaning Christians have encouraged wives to *"meet his physical needs."* You've probably heard such suggestions as, *"Remain sexually available to your husband," "Don't say no when he wants to have sex,"* and even suggestions that if a woman doesn't meet her husband's sexual desires he could be tempted to cheat.

As biblical support in 1 Corinthians 7:3-5, where the apostle Paul writes about fulfilling one another's sexual needs in marriage, and assert that wives therefore owe their husbands sex. It's true that we should meet one another's emotional needs and deepest longings in marriage.

However, what Paul actually said was, "The husband should fulfil his wife's sexual needs, and the wife should fulfil her husband's needs." The wife's needs get mentioned FIRST, so clearly God believes wives have sexual needs too and wants them met in marriage. God wants both husband and wife to experience and enjoy sexual intimacy. Sex is for BOTH spouses.

Anything beyond the missionary position is wrong.

God laid out some sexual practices as wrong in (Leviticus 18), and others are unwise because they involve a health risk or don't demonstrate love and respect. However, God gave us a lot of freedom in the marriage bed, including positions our bodies to make love.

May I say that there's nothing particularly spiritual about the missionary position, and Song of Songs shows that we can explore and experience many sensations in the marriage bed. Indeed, those of us who are older might have discovered that a different position is easier on our muscles and joints. Go ahead and try some positions to see what works best for you and your spouse. It's okay with God.

Enjoying passionate sex is indulging in the "flesh."

Several New Testament passages address living by the flesh versus living by the Spirit. Following that thinking into the sexual realm, some have concluded that little could be more flesh-like than pressing your flesh together in the act of sex? So while it's necessary for procreation and unity in marriage, maybe we shouldn't enjoy it quite so much.

However, "flesh" refers to sinful practices that emanate from physical desires. Later translations chose "sinful nature" to more accurately convey meaning. And look at the list of what comes out of that "flesh" or "sinful nature".

The Bible says, *"When you follow the desires of your sinful nature, the results are very clear: sexual immorality, impurity, lustful pleasures, idolatry, sorcery, hostility, quarrelling, jealousy, outbursts of anger, selfish ambition, dissension, division, envy, drunkenness, wild parties, and other sins like these. Let me tell you again, as I have before, that anyone living that sort of life will not inherit the Kingdom of God"* (Galatians 5:19-21).

There's nothing that even comes close to marital sexual intimacy. Think of it this way: Our flesh is involved in spiritual activities like giving to the poor, feeding the hungry, and singing praises. It's good to use our bodies to honour God according to His will, including sex in marriage.

Husbands have high sex drives, and wives don't.

Almost all of our marriage resources presume a sex-eager male and a less-interested female, leaving higher-drive wives and lower-drive husbands wondering what's wrong with them. Let me assures those couples that you are not alone. In most marriages, I believe that the wife is the higher-drive spouse.

By solely addressing the majority, we miss a substantial minority as millions of wives, whose experiences don't align with our message. We need to speak to those couples, assuring them that they are normal and providing wisdom and resources to deal with a mismatch of sex drives. Let's stop assuming who the higher-drive spouse is and deal with real marriages.

Sexual feelings before marriage are sinful.

When I was growing up, the church conveyed that it wasn't just sex outside of marriage that was wrong. Rather, sexual feelings themselves were dangerous and needed to be shut down. As a result, too many teenagers and young adults either became repressed in their sexuality all the way into their marriage or chucked the whole idea and became promiscuous instead.

But it's not the feelings themselves are not the problem, but what we do with them. God created us as sexual beings, but, wanting the best for us, provides proper parameters. We are not to have sex outside of marriage or to engage in lust: *"But I say, anyone who even looks at a woman with lust has already committed adultery with her in his heart" (Matthew 5:28).*

The truth is that we need to define lust more clearly, so that we can embrace our sexuality while keeping ourselves from sin. We should teach singles how to avoid lust and sexual sin, but their sexuality should be acknowledged, channelled and placed in the right context for a covenant marriage.

If we talk to our kids about sex, they'll have it.

If your kids never hear about sex from you, their curious minds will look for the information elsewhere. And that perspective likely won't include the values we want to teach them about sex as God created it.

This approach to parents and mentors discussing sex and their values with kids has been shown to have positive results. Research studies show that kids whose parents communicate about sex are actually less likely to engage in risky sexual behaviour and more likely to wait.

God encourages us to talk to our kids about what's in the Bible, and He didn't exclude the parts with sexual content. We must be wise about age appropriateness, but if we have a duty to teach them about God's plan for sexuality—how it's a good thing for marriage, and how to pursue holiness in this area.

Hear what the Bible says, *"How can a young person stay pure? By obeying your word,"* (Psalm 119:9), but that means they need to hear and know God's Word. Which can start with you.

Chapter 17
Show Kindness
To Your Spouse.

We teach our children to be kind to others, and then we somehow forget to follow this command ourselves. How often are our relationships marked by a lack of simple civility and thoughtfulness? Our words can be gruff and uncaring. The going out of our way to do good things for each other that characterized our dating relationships seem to fly out the window.

I'm convinced that kindness and thoughtfulness would transform our marriages. Think of the tangible difference it would make in your marital relationship to speak kindly to each other and to look for opportunities to help each other. What would your marriage look like if you both simply sought to put each other before yourself?

Taking away harshness and replacing it with kindness would thoroughly change the atmosphere and feel of your marriage.

Forgive Your Spouse. At it's best, marriage is the union of two redeemed sinners. While Christian spouses will both be experiencing conformity to the image of Christ, there will still be remaining sin in each of their lives and they will sin against each other.

What one spouse does when the other sins against them will be what defines the tenor of your marriage going forward. If you harbour grievances and anger toward your spouse for what they have done to you, do not be surprised when it begins to show in the way you interact with each other.

When one spouse hurts the other, the offender must apologize and ask for forgiveness. This is the simple act of taking responsibility for your sin and the damage it caused. Make no excuses, but instead offer an unconditional apology and ask your spouse to forgive you. Then, the offended spouse has a serious choice to make.

The truth is to forgive is not to simply say, "It's okay." What happened was not "okay" and you don't need to gloss over it with the wave of a hand. You need to forgive. This means you no longer hold this sin against them and will not bring it up again.

When you forgive another person, you are saying you will not dwell on it, will not bring it back up to your spouse, and will not talk about it with other people. To forgive is to let go of your need for mental or actual revenge and trust that this sin has been fully dealt with in the death of Jesus.

Finally Paul teaches us to walk in love towards each other. The call here is simple, yet it demands a death to self that does not come easily for us. To walk in love is for a person to put his spouse before himself and to look out for her before he looks out for himself. It is a demand to sacrifice and to do good to him even if it costs her. Love is not a mere feeling, but a settled commitment to the good of your spouse from a heart that cares deeply for him or her.

We walk in love because Christ loved us, and he gave himself up for us. If you think about everything we have walked through, especially kindness, love, and forgiveness, it models the love that

God has shown towards us in the Gospel. For the Christian spouse, you must simply look at how God has treated you in the Gospel and model that behaviour towards your spouse.

You don't need to drum up forgiveness or love from within yourself. I believe you already know what it means to be loved and forgiven in the deepest way possible. When we apply the Gospel and its implications to our marriages, I know that the possibilities for growth are endless; and what it produces will be beautiful and that is the reason this book is written.

Serious Consequences of Infidelity

Infidelity is by far one of the worst things that can transpire in marriage. Trust me, I know from personal experience! It violates everything built between you and your spouse in such a personal way.

Majority of the people who've been cheated on didn't see it coming. You now know that you've been blindsided for sure! Infidelity is like death, in more ways than one: the death of your trust, the death of your affection, the death of all the work you've done in your marriage.

There's no doubt that infidelity negatively and deeply impacts marriages in the worst way.

Consequences of infidelity:

1. Your relationship with God could suffer from a break in fellowship.

2. Having to seek forgiveness from God.

3. Having to seek forgiveness from your spouse.

4. Suffering from the emotional consequences of guilt.

5. Spending numerous hours replaying the failure.

6. Both you and your spouse suffering the emotional scars of this betrayal.

7. Countless hours in counselling.

8. Recovery will be long and painful.

9. The pain will be deeply compounded by one's own suffering and shame.

10. Your marriage will suffer a break in trust, fellowship, and intimacy.

11. You may be together, but feel excessive loneliness.

12. The reputation of your family may suffer.

13. Your kid(s) may be disappointed, confused, and may not forgive.

14. Friends & Family may be disappointed and question your integrity.

15. Job loss possibly resulting from emotional drain and the inability to focus and function.

16. Family relationships are likely to suffer and even end.

17. Divorce.

18. Some folks may shy away from you and dissolve friendships.

19. Being the bearer of such significant emotional pain to one another.

20. An unwanted child conceived.

21. Abortion of an innocent child conceived during the affair.

22. Diseases exchanged and transmitted infecting the innocent spouse.

23. Self-employed business owners may lose trust resulting in a loss of business.

24. If one is in a leadership role it might be diminished in impact.

25. Making marriage look like another bad statistic deterring people from getting married.

26. Illnesses resulting from stress, depression, anxiety, & etc.

27. Might have to start life over again.

28. Perhaps a generational curse has been created.

29. Loss of trust and intimacy (possibly forever).

30. Death from disease and/or violence (domestic).

Well, this is quite a sobering list, yes? What's even more sobering is that many people will consider these consequences and still turn a blind eye to proceed in self and spousal destruction. The fantasy is more important to them than the reality.

The biggest benefit of this list may be in helping all of us infidelity proof our marriages, by realizing the need to set up strict safeguards to ensure that we are faithful in our marital commitment. I can confidently say, if my husband and I had both known what adultery would do to us, our family, and our friends, we would have watched our wandering eyes, guarded our thought life, and avoided the situations that put us in harm's way.

I think it is important to make mention that though we SUFFERED many of the above, God saw us through and we are happily on the other side of infidelity. So it is possible, and for that I wish to give hope to marriages going through this...that you can come out thriving on the other side. However, **trust me that you rather be proactive vs. reactive! Infidelity is one of the easiest ways to damage a marriage.**

The reason infidelity is the closest thing to impossible to resolve and work through is because it completely shatters the most basic foundation of a marriage: trust.

Infidelity can collapse even the strongest bonds and is especially dangerous because it has the power to destroy your marriage. Don't cheat on your spouse, unless you're ready for some major consequences!

Things That Make for a Healthy Marriage

Every marriage contains its share of challenges. There will be difficult seasons in even the happiest of unions. It might be an overstatement to compare marriage to a rollercoaster, but even a healthy relationship is like a country road, with its twists and turns and occasional dips.

The key is how you respond to the challenges. May I challenge Christian men and women to examine their own lives and behaviour. Marriage is not an entitlement. It's a gift that too many of us have squandered. Too many couples, especially Christian couples, expect perfection. If you're going through a rough patch, is it possible you're making a mountain out of a molehill?

I've listed some criteria of healthy marriages that I would like to share them with you.

1. High levels of friendship, respect, affection, and humour.

This is defined as liking each other, being each other's best friend, doing things together; showing interest in and respect for the other's thoughts and feelings, avoiding put-downs, supporting each other's goals and aspirations, feeling affection for each other, having fun and laughter together, being number one in each other's eyes.

2. A ratio of 5:1 or better of positive to negative interactions.

This means that your relationship averages at least five pleasant, friendly, or loving experiences or periods of time for every hostile word, angry argument, or time spent feeling hurt or resentful. And 5:1 is the minimum!

3. Successful "bids for attention"

When a wife says, "Hey, listen to this!" she is trying to get her husband's attention for a conversation. If the husband keeps on scrolling through Facebook, ignoring her, he's turning away her bid for attention. If he says "Huh?" and lifts his eyes off the sports page for a second or two, he's turning toward her—a good sign.

And if he actually listens to what she has to say, that's a real connection! In successful marriages, partners turn toward each with higher percent of the time. In divorcing couples, the average is very low percent.

4. Soft starts of disagreements.

In successful marriages, disagreements are started softly, without critical, contemptuous remarks about the other person.

5. Husband accepts influence from wife.

In successful marriages, husbands accept influence from their wives. If a wife says she's afraid her husband is driving too fast and he responds in irritation, "I know what I'm doing!" this is a shaky marriage.

There must be, give and take, in a relationship. Research shows that women are accustomed to accepting influence from men. So it's crucial that men learn to do the same!

6. Respect for each other's needs, likes, dislikes, and inner life.

They ask questions to find out; they listen; they care! How did you care? I pray that you sense the urgency in my words when I remind you that next to your relationship with the Lord, the best investment you can make here on earth is the relationship with your spouse.

So much hinges on the health of our marriage. Yes, marriage is difficult. But remember, it's not designed to make us happy (though it ultimately will); it's designed to make us holy. As someone wrote, "If love were only a feeling, there would be no basis for the promise to love each other forever." In other words, the wedding vow anticipates the reality of radical difficulty. It's there in the fine print.

Chapter 18
How To Enjoy A "Happily Ever After" Marriage.

Everyone who gets married wants to enjoy a happy marriage. But too often, people wait in vain for happiness to come to them, hoping that the right spouse or the right circumstances in their marriage will somehow make them happy. The truth is that marriage can't make anyone happy, but happy people can make their marriages happy.

Enjoying a happy marriage is possible – no matter who you've married, or what circumstances you all are dealing with in your lives together – if you rely on God to help you build a happy marriage according to his design.

Here's how:

Understand that your choices significantly affect how happy you become. While your circumstances and genetics do affect the level of happiness that you experience, a significant portion of your happiness is well within your control – it comes down to the choices that you make.

So decide throughout each day to pursue happiness through intentional activities. The more you practice behaviours designed to increase your happiness, the more you'll inspire your spouse to join in, and your marriage will become happier in the process.

Pursue meaning that transcends pleasure. Realize that pursuing pleasure isn't enough in itself to make you happy; you also need to pursue meaning in order to achieve real happiness. That's because God has designed holiness (devoting yourself to God by living the way he intends) to lead to happiness.

When you move beyond the self-absorbed pursuit of pleasure for its own sake to making meaningful choices that will help you love God and others more, you naturally invite happiness into your life. **Count your blessings.** Gratitude for the many gifts that God brings into the life that you and your spouse share will strengthen your relationship with each other.

The more you give thanks to God for your blessings, the more blessings you will notice and appreciate, which will cause you to enjoy your lives more and inspire more love between you.

Make a conscious effort to count your blessings regularly, in ways such as: cutting down on complaining, keeping a written record of your blessings in a gratitude journal, going with your spouse to visit someone who has helped either one of you in the past to thank him or her, and savouring the good moments you and your spouse experience together.

Try new things. Moving out of your comfort zones to experience new adventures together keeps your relationships fresh and leads to deeper happiness in your marriage.

Some of the ways you can try new things together include: sharing a passion for an activity that both of you can enjoy doing together for fun, spicing up your sex life with new sexual positions and lovemaking locations, making new friends together, and spending your money on experiences together (like vacations and restaurant dinners) rather than material items.

Dream together. Following your dreams together will make your marriage happier by stirring optimism and empowering action in your lives. Plus, when you support each other in the process of pursuing dreams, you can accomplish more together than you could alone.

You can dream together in ways such as: envisioning what you each hope your future will be like and discussing details of it together, overcoming your fear of failure by taking steps of faith toward making your dreams come true, building a "bucket list" of experiences you hope to have together during your lifetimes, identifying dreams that are most meaningful to each of you, keeping hope alive by discussing your dreams together often, and setting goals (that are specific, measurable, achievable, realistic, and time sensitive) to help you achieve your dreams.

Celebrate each other. When you make a habit of celebrating the positive moments that you and your spouse share, you avoid falling into the unhappy trap of taking each other for granted and instead fuel mutual admiration and honour that will contribute to happiness in your marriage.

Celebrating each other inspires and motivates each other to be your best selves as you relate to each other. Ways you can celebrate each other include: complimenting each other for positive words and actions you notice every day, responding to each other's good news with excitement, incorporating fun and loving sex into your lives on a regular basis, enjoying listening to music together often, expressing affection freely (such as through hugs, kisses, and backrubs), and serving each other regularly through acts of kindness (such as preparing special meals or taking on chores and errands for your spouse when he or she is especially busy).

Attune your spirits. Pursuing spiritual intimacy with each other will make your marriage happier by drawing you both closer to the ultimate source of joy: God.

You can do so in ways that include: incorporating spiritual disciplines (such as praying, reading the Bible, and participating in church) into your lives together, openly and honestly discussing details of how God is working in both of your lives, and responding gracefully to each other's faults as God does.

Add value to others. When you work together to assist or cheer up people whom God leads you to help or encourage, you double your impact for good and make your marriage happier as you make others happier. Keep in mind that, as Christian spouses, God has ordained you to serve others as a team.

Some of the ways you can add value to others include: making a list of kind acts you can do together (of different varieties, including some that you all can do anonymously), reviewing your experiences together afterward, mentoring other spouses to help them have better marriages, and sponsoring an impoverished child together.

Overcome the biggest hurdles to happiness as a couple. Those hurdles include: depending on money to make you happy, comparing yourselves to others, holding on to pride, obsessing over the past pain and regrets, fixating on the future rather than living fully in the present, and focusing what you *don't* have rather than what you *do* have.

When you overcome those hurdles, you can enjoy a happy marriage that endures through life's uncertainties with the certainty of God-given joy. I do believe that the desire that you have for a lifelong, intimate marriage is a God-given one that reflects His plan for marriage. But when you look around, you see many marriages that either don't last or aren't close and happy relationships.

Despite the divorce and marital tension that are so prevalent, marriages in which spouses live "happily ever after" aren't just found in fairy tales. They do exist – and you and your spouse can enjoy one, if you approach marriage the way God intends.

Here's how you and your spouse can enjoy a marriage that really is a happy one, today and every day after: **Find your "one."** Loving Jesus must be your number one priority in life if you're going to become the kind of person God wants you to become and be able to give and receive love in your marriage the way you should.

So reach out to Jesus with all of your heart, devoting the best of your time and energy to pursuing a closer relationship with Him. Place your relationship with Jesus at the centre of your life and revolve everything else around it.

Find your "two." If you're not yet married and are looking for a spouse, search for a spouse carefully, in ways that honour God.

Don't even consider marrying someone who's not a Christian because you can't ever truly be compatible with someone who doesn't share your spiritual connect with Jesus, and marrying a non-Christian can only bring misery into your life that will grow.

Beyond choosing a person who's a Christian, you should also look for someone who shares common interests with you, whose personality fits well with yours, and to whom you're physically attracted. Don't rush the process, and don't settle for less than God's best for you simply to marry by a certain time.

Move a relationship with a potential spouse through first gear.

In first gear, when your relationship with a potential future spouse is just beginning, work to get to know each other well and build a strong foundation of friendship. Rather than spending time alone, try to spend most of your time together with groups of people.

If your discover that you're not interested in taking the relationship to the next gear, then don't lead the other person on; be honest about how you feel to avoid hurting that person more deeply later on.

Move a relationship with a potential spouse through second gear.

In second gear, as you sense God blessing your friendship, you can spend more time alone together. But continue to guard your heart, and avoid discussing marriage at this point.

However, ask yourself questions like: "Is this person becoming more like Christ?", "Does this person have a strong and growing character?", "Does this person have the right kind of friends?", "Is this person responsible – financially, relationally, emotionally, intellectually?", "Is our attraction increasing?", and "Are we helping each other grow closer to God, rather than drawing each other away from Him?"

If the person you're dating isn't helping you move closer to God or isn't right for you, break up with him or her as soon as you know.

Move a relationship with a potential spouse through third gear.

In third gear, you should discuss the possibility of getting married and explore it with the help of prayer, advice from mentors, getting to know each other's families, and talking openly about how each of you have been both hurt and helped in life and what dreams each of you are hoping will come true in your lives.

Don't hesitate to break up if God isn't clearly leading the two of you to get married; it's better to end the relationship (and grieve and heal) before making a lifetime commitment than to marry when you know you shouldn't.

Move into fourth gear: engagement. If it's clear to you both that marriage is where God is leading your relationship, then set a wedding date. But use the time during your engagement to plan your *marriage* – not just your *wedding*.

Participate in premarital counselling, and discuss issues about which you'll have to make decisions about together in married life, like: career choices, where you'll live once you're married, how you'll share and manage your finances, your philosophy for bearing and raising children, which church you'll be a part of together, and how you plan to grow spiritually together.

Continue to protect your sexual purity during your entire engagement until you're actually married, so you can enjoy God's best during your marriage. The fifth gear is marriage itself!

Pursue sexual purity. Keep in mind that you can't have premarital sex without consequences (physical, emotional, and spiritual), so your future marriage will be affected in significant ways if you and your future spouse have sex before your wedding.

Realize that you can't have premarital sex without intimacy, either, since God designed sex to develop intimacy between people, so if you end up breaking up with the person you had sex with it, the breakup will hurt badly. Ask God to help you make and keep a commitment to abstain from sexual behaviour of any kind until your wedding night.

You'll gain many benefits if you do, including trust between you and your spouse (if you compromise sexually before marriage, you may compromise after marriage by having affairs) and an exciting sex life (that you'll never have to compare to the thrill of dangerous sex before marriage and are free to build with real intimacy between you).

Set clear boundaries of behaviour in your relationship to guard your sexual purity (such as no sleepovers) and ask some trusted friends to hold you both accountable to respect those boundaries. **Identify sins and wounds and pursue repentance and healing.** Both you and the person you're considering marrying need to confess sins to God regularly, repent of them, and accept God's forgiveness and strength to make better decisions.

You all should also talk honestly with God and each other about the emotional wounds you've suffered in life, and seek God's healing for them, perhaps through Christian counselling. This will help you both begin married life as healthy as possible.

Keep passion alive after you're married. Every new day that God gives you and your spouse during your marriage, pursue each other like you did when you were dating, seeking to learn something new about each other, and nurture the passion and deepen the intimacy between you. Don't keep sins or secrets from each other; confess them to each other and pray for each other regularly.

Submit to God together.

Rather than trying to convince each other to make decisions that either you want or that your spouse wants, commit to seeking God's will together regularly and basing your decisions on the guidance He gives you. Learn how to pray together, listen carefully to each other and to God, and work through conflicts with love and respect.

Chapter 19
Why You Can't Ignore The Truth In Marriage.

I like to believe I think the best about people and generally believe things will work out. Problems will resolve, issues will be settled, and life will return to normalcy. I dream above the current limitations of today.

This all sounds wonderful, right? It sounds like I'm an optimist and my belief system works for me and others, right? Not so fast. Even as we speak, I have several warning lights on the dash of my car. Why are they on and what am I doing about them? You guessed it. Nothing. Why?

Magical thinking---the belief that nothing too bad is going to happen, that all things will magically work out. I can relax when using magical thinking, imagining the situation corrected. I'll get around to getting those warning lights checked in time before any calamity arises.

While I might be right and escape any serious problems, I might also be very, very wrong. The warning lights are there for a reason—to warn me.

While my example thinking may be fairly begin, people use this thinking error far too often to their own demise.

Consider Jessica who is married to Samson, a problem drinker. "Problem drinker," by the way, may be a euphemism for "alcoholic." It may be, in fact probably is, a way for Jessica to use magical thinking, avoiding the repercussions of calling the problem something more serious than it is.

I have been talking to Jessica for weeks about the pain she was feeling about Samson's increasing irresponsible drinking and the impact on her and their children. We had discussed at length how she was growing increasingly frightened that he might have been unfaithful to her, had been spending more money on drinking, had increased tolerance for alcohol, and had disregarded other boundaries they had established.

The warning signs had grown increasingly strong, bright and loud. Not surprisingly, however, both Jessica and Samson found ways to silence and dim those warning signs. Samson had scolded her for worrying about him. He shifted the blame to her, saying she was worrying over nothing. Perhaps what was a bit more surprising was Jessica's defence of him when talking with me.

"Of course, I don't like it," she said. "But, he tells me there is nothing to worry about, claiming it's simply a stressful time at work and there is no harm to his stopping off for a few beers."

"What about your fears that he could have been unfaithful?" I asked.

"He tells me it's all in my head," she shared. "I do tend to worry needlessly."

"He continues to violate your agreements Jessica ," I said, increasing my confrontation. "He promises to get better," she said, becoming increasingly defensive.

I could see that Jessica was caught up in magical thinking and wasn't ready to see the truth. She was caught between Samson's protests, her own anxiety, and now my strong words. Samson, too, was using denial and magical thinking to continue his lifestyle.

He was not ready to face his downward spiral and the impact his drinking had on his marriage, health, and family life. Both Samson and Jessica were headed for disaster. Let's consider why they use magical thinking and what they and loved ones can do about it:

First, magical thinking is just that--magical. While there are tempting bits and pieces of truth in magical thinking, and it is so tempting to embrace it, magical thinking is overly hopeful and lacks the grounding necessary to really face problems and solve them. Many problems don't naturally resolve themselves, but in fact need solid, firm confrontation and radical change.

Second, magical thinking leaves us vulnerable to worse problems. Ignoring the warning lights on my car clearly leaves me vulnerable to worse problems. (I'm taking my car to the shop this week, by the way!) Many problems don't automatically disappear but become worse. Doctors, dentists, psychologists, and car mechanics, to name a few, are there for our help, waiting for us to reach out for assistance. **They can help keep small problems, small.**

Third, magical thinking stops us from effective problem-solving. Scripture implores us to use wisdom in our lives, not magical thinking. *"If any of you lacks wisdom, you should ask God." (James 1:5)* *Then hear this, "The fear of the Lord is the beginning of knowledge, but fools despise wisdom and instruction." (Proverbs 1:7)* **We are never to ignore problems, but rather to seek the Lord, wisdom and wise instruction.**

Fourth, ending magical thinking takes work. Yes, facing magical thinking and allowing reality to come crashing in, means facing difficulty. Facing the truth sets us free, after it hurts and challenges us. After the hurt and hard work become real, we have possibilities.

Once Jessica faces the hard truths about Samson's drinking, they have the possibilities of a sober, joy-filled life that is not possible now. Facing truth requires change—after change comes hope for a new, prosperous life.

Finally, embrace healthy, grounded positive magical thinking. Scripture tells us, *"Yet God has made everything beautiful for its own time. He has planted eternity in the human heart, but even so, people cannot see the whole scope of God's work from beginning to end." (Ecclesiastes 3:11).* God has allowed us to dream far above our current realities, but we must be in step with His plans for us.

Are you ready face the truth and the reality of your life and make necessary changes? Are you ready to face uncertainty in exchange for a positive, joyful future? That is why this book is written for you.

Chapter 20
Pray Against Satanic Attack.

H ave you ever think or imagine that your husband struggles with attack daily.

He may not talk with you about it, but the struggle is real. Sometimes the attack is from his own flesh.

Sometimes it's a natural consequence of living in a sinful world. And sometimes it's a direct assault from his "adversary the devil [who] prowls around like a roaring lion, seeking someone to devour" (1 Peter 5:8). You can grab hold of a strategy outlined in Scripture to thwart Satan's attack against your husband.

Scripture commands believers to "be strong in the Lord and in the strength of his might" and to "put on the whole armour of God" so that we can "stand against the schemes of the devil." Furthermore, we are told that "we do not wrestle against flesh and blood, but against the rulers, against the authorities, against the cosmic powers over this present darkness, against the spiritual forces of evil in the heavenly places" (Ephesians 6:10-13).

When you, as wives, suit up in the armour of God (which basically means to cover ourselves in the character of Christ and pray in the Spirit at all times), we can—through faith and God's Word – "extinguish all the flaming darts of the evil one" (verse 16). Those flaming darts are hurled at several areas of your husband's life. So here are 10 areas of your husband's life to pray against Satan's attack:

His Drive for Success:

Most men want to feel successful and do well in their careers, but some take it too far and become obsessed with climbing the corporate ladder to the harm of family and friends. This is the lure of status, prestige, and power. The world will tell him this is important and this is where he finds his value and significance.

Pray that your husband clearly sees his worth and significance in Christ, not in the accolades from the workplace or an area in which he excels. Ask God to press upon him to want to succeed as a man of God, and to realize he will be held accountable before God not for how many hours he put into the office but for how he invested in what God gave him (his wife, family, and talents to serve the body of Christ).

Lets Pray:

Lord, cultivate in my husband a drive and desire to serve You more than any other person or thing. Close his ears to how the world around him defines success and whisper to Him how You define it – to do justice, and to love kindness, and to walk humbly with his God according to your word in (Micah 6:8).

His Desire for More:

Is your man content? If so, that's an area that Satan wants to undermine by convincing him he needs more. More electronic gadgets, more sound in his home theatre, more stuff in his garage, more toys out on the lake, and so on.

Scripture says *"But godliness with contentment is great gain, for we brought nothing into the world, and we cannot take anything out of the world"* (1 Timothy 6:6-7).

Lord, help my husband to be content with all You have given him, and to ignore Satan's – and the world's – lure that he must have more. Help him to be eternally minded, not wanting to store up treasures on earth, but desiring treasure in heaven where neither moth nor rust destroys, and where thieves do not break in and steal. Matthew 6:19-20). In Jesus name. Amen

His Belief That He Can Do it Alone

If Satan can isolate your man he can more easily divide him. Your husband may have call this area of a man's life "The Rambo Reflex" and said "It's the error of thinking a man doesn't need help, doesn't need advice, and can handle all of his problems on his own. *Besides, there's no one I can trust anyway*, he thinks. That's a lie. And it's from the pit of hell."

I believe that God designed us to live in community. First and foremost, He gave you, (the Wife) as an helper, to your husband, (Genesis 2:18). God also designed the church to come alongside one another and support each other. Pray that your husband will receive help, friendship, support, and encouragement from his brothers in Christ (if he is a believer) or from godly men who care about him.

Lord, surround my husband with men of God who will care deeply about him, reach out to him, and remind him he is not alone in Jesus name. Amen.

His Eyes and Thought-Life

May I remind you that because your husband he's a man, he is visually wired in a way that you, as a woman, will never fully understand. Therefore, the temptation for sexual lust is waiting for him around every corner. Every man faces sexual temptation whether it's in print, digitally, or a real woman he sees from a distance or works with closely.

Your husband is bombarded with sexual images every day on television, on freeway billboards, or on social media. What once was available only by walking into an adult theatre or through purchasing an adult magazine, is now easily accessible on any laptop or smartphone. So, pray for him to surrender his temptations to God as soon as lustful thoughts begin to enter his mind.

Lord, guard my husband's eyes, filter his thoughts, and convict his heart so that he immediately surrenders to You whatever causes him to begin to lust. Keep his mind pure and don't let images stay in his mind and begin to lure his heart away in Jesus name Amen.

His Fear of Failure

Men dread failure and appearing weak or not having what it takes, so the enemy aims his attack at your husband's self-confidence and character. He also feels the attack when it comes to his sense of responsibility ("I'm a horrible provider," "I'll never get ahead of these bills," "My wife and kids deserve better," "I'll never achieve my dreams").

Someone wrote: "The mass of men lead lives of quiet desperation. What is called resignation is confirmed desperation. From the desperate city, you go into the desperate country, and have to console yourself with the bravery of minks and muskrats. A stereotyped but unconscious despair is concealed even under what are called the games and amusements of mankind. There is no play in them, for this comes after work."

Lets pray:

Lord, may my husband find his sense of worth not in what he does (or in what he succeeds at), but in Whom he knows. Remind him that as he brings his heart before You, You are pleased, regardless of how he performs. And help him to remember that He is "fearfully and wonderfully" made (Psalm 139:14), and whatever he fails at is part of Your overall design to shape his character and teach him to lean on You for his strength in Jesus name. Amen.

His Fear of Weakness.

Fear can paralyze a man from doing what he knows deep in his heart he's supposed to do: Stand up to his controlling boss, confront the dad of his son's friend who let them do something foolish, risk having that argument with his wife, take his family to church, talk to his neighbour about Christ, and so on.

God has not given your husband the spirit of fear, but of power and love and self-control (2 Timothy 1:7).

Lord, Your Word says "Perfect love casts out fear" (John 4:18). Help my husband to love You perfectly and therefore, to trust You immensely so that there is no room for fear. Make him a man of courage because he trusts in You in Jesus name. Amen.

His Tendency Toward Complacency

The attack of complacency comes in many different forms: neglecting priorities and responsibilities, feeling comfortable with the status quo in his job when he's capable of more, or watching the house fall down around his family while he pops another beer and watches three more hours of sports.

Complacency also occurs in his marriage when he stops trying and adopts an "it's good enough" attitude. *Lord, don't let my husband be content with status quo. Help him to give to You the lure to be lazy, the feeling that he's tired of trying, and the sense of defeat that leads to complacency in Jesus name. Amen.*

His Male Ego

Some men are raised to believe they're supposed to be bullies, tough to the point where they don't have any empathy or sympathy. It's a "big boys don't cry" attitude and it's based in pride and a lack of compassion. "Never display any weakness" they are taught. And every issue is solved best by a fist-fight.

This may not be your man. But the temptation is there to default into the tough guy who must prove his manliness through brute force. Pray that your husband embraces the fruits of the Spirit that will make him more like Christ. *Lord, help my husband to surrender to Your Spirit's control and develop Your character, particularly love, joy, peace, patience, kindness, goodness, faithfulness, gentleness, and self-control in Jesus name. Amen. (Galatians 5:22-23).*

His Ability to Go Silent or Passive

According to a wife to the husband, she said there is a pastor who has led men's groups for more than 20 years – the attack sounds something like this: "Just don't say anything," "Just don't get involved," "It's not your problem," "It won't make a difference anyway," "No one wants to hear what you have to say," "Don't you have more important things to do?"

Lord, don't let Satan tempt my man to resign into passivity and not take a stand. Give him a zealousness for the truth and to be active, involved, and present in the affairs of his marriage, family, workplace, and church in Jesus name. Amen.

His Heart for God

I often hear from wives whose husbands once loved and served God with a passion, but something happened to steal their hearts away. Sometimes it's PTSD, a slow-growing addiction, the lure of another woman, another "high", or another lifestyle. Pray that your husband's heart will constantly seek God, and never settle for less.

Lord, keep my husband's heart close to you. Don't let him entertain anything that will divide his heart and cause him to compromise his faith, his marriage, his parenting, his work, or his health. Convince him that his greatest "high" and his deepest sense of fulfilment will only be found in You. Be his joy, his Rock, his Loving Father, his Warrior King and his heart's delight in Jesus name. Amen.

Chapter 21
Signs Your Marriage Is Heading For Trouble.

Every day we hear heart breaking stories of marriages failing and falling apart. These couples had the greatest intentions when starting out, but somehow, life left their marriages broken and their hearts tattered. When we hear these gut-wrenching stories, we often think, "Please, Lord… don't let that happen to my marriage".

While it would be impossible (and arrogant!) to assume that every marriage follows a particular pattern, I would argue that many marriages that are in trouble show one or more of the signs that I'm going to mention in this book.

Do you see these happening in your marriage? For the health of your marriage, I encourage you to read through this chapter with an open and honest heart.

May I let you know that I purposely based these *"marriage warning signs"* around scriptural truths. If you see this happening in your marriage, I highly encourage you to meditate on these biblical truths for more wisdom and application for your particular situation! Also, physical or mental abuse are definite signs of a marriage in trouble. I'd advise that you seek immediate help should this describe your marriage.

One of signs your marriage is heading for trouble is when you don't desire to serve your spouse or to put them first. "Serving our spouses": that phrase seems almost taboo or, at the very least counter-cultural. And yet, we are called to sacrificially love our spouses (Ephesians 5) everyday, whether that's physically serving them or allowing their opinions to be as valuable as our own (Philippians 2:3-4) when making decisions.

In fact, sacrificial love, which includes letting our spouses have their way, or choosing to bless them without a guarantee of return. May I remind you that this is the exact type of love that we signed up to do when we chose to get married according to (1 Corinthians 13).

At this point, I hear you say "Why should I serve my spouse when my spouse do XYZ, when my spouse don't treat me right, or when I know my spouse won't serve me back in return?" But here's the thing: rending yourself unable to love you spouse "until" (until he or she treat you correctly, etc.) means that you are short changing the beautiful example of sacrificial love that God designed for marriage.

Let me say this that, the bottom line is the inability to unconditionally serve your spouse will severely limit the closeness between the two of you and stifle God's desire to use marriage to grow you in holiness. Your spouse doesn't have to "deserve" your unconditional love in order for you to give it. In fact, that's the very definition of unconditional love and the foundation of grace itself.

In fact, there are many, many times in marriage where we must choose to love our spouses not out of emotion or condition, but because of our decision to love them as Christ has called us to. These moments are a very real reminder that we aren't really serving our spouses in marriage but God Himself!

Marriage can be selfish and very much "tit for tat," but it will also be stifled and headed for trouble when performed under these conditions. May I say that if you see signs of this in your marriage, consider what Paul, an apostle of Christ Jesus say in the book of Ephesians.

"And further, submit to one another out of reverence for Christ. For wives, this means submit to your husbands as to the Lord...As the church submits to Christ, so you wives should submit to your husbands in everything. For husbands, this means love your wives, just as Christ loved the church. He gave up his life for her to make her holy and clean, washed by the cleansing of God's word...In the same way, husbands ought to love their wives as they love their own bodies. For a man who loves his wife actually shows love her himself. .. So again I say, each man must love his wife as he loves himself, and the wife must respect her husband." (Ephesians 5:22, 24-26, 28, 33)

Hear what the Bible say, *"An unmarried man can spend his time doing the Lord's work and thinking how to please him. but a married man has to think about his earthly responsibilities and how to please his wife. His interests are divided. In the same way, a woman who is no longer married or has never been married can be devoted to the Lord and holy in body and in spirit. But a married woman has to think about her earthly responsibilities and how to please her husband."* (1 Corinthians 7:32-34).

Another sign that your marriage is heading for trouble is that you care less and less about your spouse's opinions or desires. Truth be told, sometimes our spouses annoy us! They may drive us crazy with their opinions or what may feel like a demand on our time. We all have moments where we'd rather push our spouse's opinions aside and think, "I have to do what everyone else wants all day long at work, school, etc. At least in my own home, I want to have my own way!"

While I'm not advocating that we dismiss our feelings or don't give validity to our emotions, it's dangerous to a marriage when we habitually choose to not weigh our spouse's opinions as important as our own. Why? Because friendship is the foundation of every marriage. A strong friendship isn't self-seeking, but seeks to bless and help the other person, which sometimes results in sacrificing our own opinions and desires in order to maintain peace or demonstrate love. (1 Corinthians 13).

That's why when we dismiss our spouse's feelings as unimportant, we are hurting the friendship with our spouse, and by default, damaging our marriage. Be careful of this secret marriage destroyer! It is a sneaky tactic the enemy uses to slowly erode even the strongest marriages!

Hear what the scriptures say for more insight: *"Love is patient and kind. Love is not jealous or boastful or proud or rude. It does not demand its own way."* (1 Corinthians 13:4-5). *"Don't be concerned for your own good but for the good of others." (1 Corinthians 10:24). "Be humble, thinking of others as better than yourselves. Don't look out only for your own interest, but take an interest in others too." (Philippians 2:3-4).*

This is a sign that your marriage is heading for trouble when unresolved conflict has built in your marriage and forgiveness seems difficult. It's normal for arguments to happen in marriage. We are, after all, two imperfect beings living together in tight quarters (often with other little people adding to our stress)!

But the real question is, "What do we do with those conflicts?" I think of unresolved tension in marriage like a pair of really dirty eyeglasses. Every time we have an argument or issue between us, our glasses (the lens of how we see each other) can get clouded and covered over with smudges, dirt and other debris.

If we don't remove those "smudges" immediately through forgiveness and reconciliation, it becomes harder to see our spouses clearly (and it certainly becomes difficult to love and serve them unconditionally)! When these lenses are clouded, we don't want to forgive because it seems too difficult, too extreme. That one little issue we had last week has compounded with that other issue from today.

The truth is, that reoccurring thing that drives us crazy! and before we know it, our hearts have shut down and our marriage is slowly dying. As hard as it seems, we must get to the root of our emotions and deal with these issues quickly with our spouses. We can't let things linger because of this compounding effect.

We must create the habit of dealing with these issues immediately and moving on so that our marriages can operate freely and not be smothered by unresolved conflict. While these Bible verses speak about conflict in friendship, they certainly are applicable to marriage since friendship is the base of a strong marriage.

They speak about the importance of forgiving quickly for the sake of peace, and of the importance of grace. The Bible says, *"Always be humble and gentle. Be patient with each other, making allowance for each other's faults because of your love. "(Ephesians 4:2).*

Hear this, *"Don't let the sun go down while you are still angry, for anger gives a foothold to the devil... Get rid of all bitterness, rage, anger, harsh words, and slander, as well as all types of evil behaviour. Instead, be kind to each other, tender hearted, forgiving one another, just as God through Christ has forgiven you." (Ephesians 4:26-27, 31-32).*

You must, *"Watch out that no poisonous root of bitterness grows up to trouble you, corrupting many." (Hebrews 12:15). "Love prospers when a fault is forgiven, but dwelling on it separates close friends." (Proverbs 17:9). "An offended friend is harder to win back than a fortified city. Arguments separate friends like a gate locked with bars." (Proverbs 18:19). "(Love) is not irritable, and it keeps no record of being wronged."* (1 Corinthians 13:5).

When Physical intimacy is non-existent or done with a lustful heart, that is an indication that your marriage is heading for trouble. I've found out in marriage that husband and wife sex life is a good indicator of their overall marital health. Do you find these aspects true in your marriage too? Consider this.

When husband and wife are tired and too busy for intimate time together, their marriage just doesn't seem as close as it should be. The truth is that When there aren't huge emotional barriers between husband and wife, sex is easy and it is a time of deep emotional connection.

Furthermore, I've also seen how sex can be a beautiful balm of reconciliation when husband and wife going through tough times. Honestly, many times, it feel like sexual intimacy "resets" the connection in my marriage. I share this to say that sex is intended to be an emotional (not just physical) investment in each other, and when a couple reduces it down to a physical act (or they don't make love regularly, they are short-changing their marital growth and connection.

Many of us let this aspect of marriage slowly erode, and quite frankly, it's easy to do so! Besides being "too busy" or "too tired," here are some other potential reasons why physical intimacy may be lacking. For instance we ignore sex because we are no longer attracted to our spouse because of physical changes they've undergone.

I know that many have been emotionally wounded in other areas (by our spouse or others) and sex seems unthinkable. Pornography or affairs have invaded the marriage and broken trust. The truth is that we have sex with our spouse, but the intimacy is gone and sex simply has become a physical release devoid of relational connection.

Let me encourage you because we can't allow the enemy to use our busy-ness or our emotional scars to keep our marriage from this most vital form of connection. Sex is important to God (the entire book of the Song of Solomon is about this physical connection between a husband and wife!) and he encourages us to "keep the marriage bed pure" (Hebrews 13:4) and to "not abstain from each other" (1 Corinthians 7:5). I believe we must make sexual connection with our spouses a priority in order for our marriages to thrive.

When you're no longer making regular, intentional investments in your marriage, your marriage is heading for trouble. The truth is that we enter marriage with hearts full of hope and excitement because we've spent hours investing in our relationship (think date nights, time alone to talk, and many things done together during courtship).

Then we get married, and suddenly as the years go by (and we become distracted by other good things like a career, kids, or even ministry), our marriage may not seem as bright and shiny with optimism anymore. In fact, it may seem lacking in vitality, force or conviction (that is) uninspired and simply limp along as we focus the bulk of our emotional energies toward other pursuits.

That's why date nights and regular scheduled time alone together are so important! We must make intentional investments in our relationship should we want them to stay vibrant and growing. *Consider this and do your thoughts, actions and schedule demonstrate that you've allowed a career, kids (or other potentially good things) to come before your marriage?*

It's so easy to let this happen! And we can come up with a thousand excuses, but we must find the creative ways to intentionally invest in our marriages. You need to intentionally invest in your marriage such simple act of taking 15 minutes to chat each day, plan regular date night, plan weekends away/vacations. Invest in other intentional time together (such as participating in a hobby or home improvement projects together)

The Bible also tells us to *"give honour to marriage and remain faithful to one another in marriage." Hebrews 13:4).* We must nurture our relationships in order to honour them and to stay faithful What to Do When You Discover That Your Marriage Exhibits These Signs I know these are heavy and difficult-to-discuss topics! Please know that I'm praying for you if you've read those and realized that, yes, your marriage may be headed for trouble.

Chapter 22
May I Encourage You To Take These Next Steps?

1. Pray for clarity and deep understanding of what's going on. Ask God for His wisdom about what's really going on in your marriage!

2. Admit to your part in contributing to these situations. As the old saying goes, "It takes two to tango." Yes, I know that your spouse plays a part but you probably play a role too. I know we don't like to think that, but we have to be truthful.

3. Receive His forgiveness and hope for your marriage. God wants to forgive us and to restore our marriages! There is always, always, always hope.

4. Lay aside the blame you feel for your spouse and ask God to help you love them "despite." This takes time and perhaps many humble pleas from a broken heart, but allow God

to show you little things you can do each day to love your spouse despite his/her flaws.

Continue to process the emotions with God, repeating these steps (and asking a wise friend or counsellor for help, if necessary). This is not easy! And it won't be solved with a quick-fix solution. We must persevere through the process of making huge changes, taking baby steps toward the goal. We're all given a choice everyday as to whether we will work to grow or to destroy our marriages.

I know these issues can seem huge and insurmountable! But if you find yourself seeing several signs that your marriage may be headed for trouble, *don't be overwhelmed by the huge mess you may see.* Get help and make those first baby steps today toward hope and healing.

Reasons to be Forgiving and Patient with Your Spouse.

She was temperamental on that particular afternoon after she came back from work. With too little sleep the night before and too much office work, my wife, " Oladunni " was a bit edgy. I could sense that she was not as easy going as usual. I was tempted to react to her but thought better of it.

That said, I've had my days as well. I can certainly pile too much on my plate and then complain when the deadlines loom near. I can procrastinate and then complain loudly. At those times I am reactive and unusually touchy. In each situation my wife and I have a policy: *No one from outside of our home or any situation must cause misunderstanding for us in the house.*

Here is how one woman describes this exercise:

"When my husband comes home in the evening, the first thing I do is greet him warmly and then give him a little time to settle into the evening. He is sometimes irritable, sometimes cranky. Sometimes he's had a great day. Either way, I see around his momentary mood. I treat him the way he wants to be treated. I see this as an act of loving him well."

You might mistakenly see this as enabling bad behaviour. That certainly is not the intent of this exercise. Rather, it is to recognize that we are not always on our best behaviour. We are sometimes very, very human. Many times, in our humanness we are less than our best and our behaviour has little to do with others. In other words, we cannot expect people to always be on their best behaviour. We don't expect that from us; we cannot expect it from others.

The truth is that *people deserve our understanding*. Yes, that's true. People deserve our understanding. We must take time to step back, consider what they are going through and why they might be behaving the way they do. Are they under unusual stress? Are they fighting a fierce, inner battle? Be understanding.

People are more than their current behaviour. We all are a composite of many parts. Our current behaviour is simply one part of who we are. Consider that when your mate is irritable, this is an expression of something deeper taking place. What is it that they are unable to express directly and perhaps in a healthier manner?

People can offer us understanding as well. The understanding you offer will often come back to you. The generosity and grace you offer will likely come back to you in other ways. People will see you as a grace-filled individual and treat you accordingly. Certainly you are needing the understanding others wish from you.

People need us to see their deeper issues. Irritability is often a manifestation of something deeper taking place. Take time to see people's faults as a disguised expression of deeper pain. Care enough to love people well and see around their faults.

"Love is patient; love is kind"(1 Corinthians 13). Finally, *people will often behave according to our expectations.* Have you noticed that people will often respond according to the way we treat them. If you dispense grace and patience, people often respond more favourably than if we treat them with impatience.

Chapter 23

Small Things That
Can Break Trust
In Your Marriage.

Truth be told, trust is the core of a marriage. A thriving marriage is built upon godly commitment. While every husband and every wife will surely make mistakes year after year, when those mistakes cause distrust to build, the marriage slowly erodes.

Sadly, there are some who think they can keep from doing the "big" stuff that would break marital trust (i.e. having an affair) but they fail to see the "small" things that are slowly eroding the trust in their marriage.

What is trust exactly?

Trust is the belief that your spouse is concerned about your overall well-being and makes decisions while acting with your best interest at heart. It's the belief that your spouse keeps his or her promises while attempting to live up to one another's expectations as best as humanly possible. Trust serves as the foundation for a healthy marriage and allows spouses to be vulnerable with one another, feeling safe and secure within their marriage.

So how is trust broken?

Trust is broken when a spouse puts his or her own needs and desires ahead of what's best for their spouse and marriage. Also, trust is damaged when spouses break their promises and spousal expectations.

We are all familiar with the well-known ways to break trust by lying and cheating, again those "big" things. However, what about the "small" day-to-day things we do that destroy trust? The ones that can be very easy to miss, or that we don't even associate with trust. Trust is essential to understand, because no truly healthy marriage can thrive in its absence.

What are some of these "small" things? Here are things that some may think are small, but that can be eroding the very core of your marital trust.

1. You're Always Late

Being a person your spouse can count on is an essential part of building trust. If you never show up when you say you will, or text when you say you will, you're sabotaging that trust. Being on time is a challenge for some, but it's absolutely something you can work on. It's a small way to let your spouse know that you're reliable.

2. You're Judgmental

If you're a judgmental spouse, you could be sabotaging the trust in your marriage. Judgmental spouses are not easy to confide in, especially when it comes to deep, personal sharing. There could be things your spouse has never told you, simply because they fear you will judge them.

3. You Lack Self-Awareness

Do you know people who seem to lack a complete sense of who they are? They say things like, "I'm the nicest person you'll ever meet," and they mean it. But in your head you're thinking, "Um, stop lying to yourself." Or, they say, "I'm a really motivated, active person," and you're think, "Girl, you've been on the couch for 15 years." These people are hard to trust because they seem like liars, even if they mean or believe what they say. If you're talking the talk, make sure you're walking the walk.

4. You Don't Express Your Feelings

If you don't express your feelings, and go deep, emotionally, you're creating an imbalance of trust. If your spouse trusts you with some really strong feelings, and the most intimate details of their lives, they trust you. When you don't do the same, it becomes clear that you don't feel the same. Trust involves a give and take. It may take you time to learn to open up and share your feelings, but its required work for both spouses.

5. You Don't Listen

Your spouse is not going to trust you with their feelings if you don't listen. To be a trustworthy spouse is to be a person your spouse can confide in. That means you have to learn to listen without interrupting, changing the subject, not hearing, or not giving your spouse's words consideration.

6. You Hate On Their Friends and Family

You can't control who your spouse chooses to have in their life, and constant negativity will just cause stressful situations. Make your feelings clear, but don't entertain hating on folks. Now if their friends and/or family are truly toxic or dangerous to your spouse or yourself then it is time to take action to remove these individuals from your inner circle.

7. You're Shady

Being shady is such an annoying trait, but your spouse needs to be able to trust, with a reasonable amount of certainty, that you'll be where you say you will be and do what you say you will do, even if those things are seemingly unimportant to you.

8. You Don't Do Your Share

Doing your share of the housework may not seem like it impacts trust, but it is absolutely part of being reliable. If you're not holding up your end of your responsibilities, your spouse could easily feel like they can't count on you (trust you) to do other things like "How can I trust you to take care of a baby/home/etc when I can't even trust you to do your share of the dishes?"

9. You Have a Temper

If your spouse has a temper, they're breaking trust in the marriage. People don't like to tell things to those with tempers. They keep secrets and avoid doing things that might set off tempers. This is a level of emotional and literal dishonesty that others have had to maintain to keep themselves safe from spousal anger.

10. You're Super Emotional

Being super emotional isn't necessarily a bad thing. And it's also not always something you can control. But unfortunately, the people who love super emotional spouses sometimes find it easier to keep things from them rather than make them upset. This can have a negative impact on the trust in a marriage, from both spouses' perspectives.

11. You're Sneaky

You leave without saying where you're going. You sneak in really late at night. You whisper when you talk on the phone. You don't like to talk about your day, what you did, or where you were. You don't necessarily have to stop doing these things, and they don't necessarily mean you're not trustworthy BUT now consider when you add them all together; they sure do make you *look* sneaky and suspect.

Opening up a little about the life you lead when you two are together will help tremendously by providing insight to your spouse. Hopefully you notice some room for improvement in your marriage and make some positive changes, because nothing feels better than having a spouse who is your rock and I know this to be true from experience!

Chapter 24

Things Every Married Couple Should Do.

"You've got to make time to invest in your marriage." If you're married, it's likely you've heard that phrase at least once. In fact, I was visiting a good friend recently and we were talking about our respective marriages when that topic came up.

The conversation we were having revolved around the idea that people are constantly telling young married couples to "invest in their marriage" without explaining what on earth that actually means. While it sounds like a noble idea, the concept of "investing in your marriage" can seem so far away for many couples, particularly during the first decade of marriage.

For instance, think about all that is going on during those first few years of your marriage. If you're anything like us, most likely, you're raising young children, sleep deprived, worn out from work, all the while trying to survive financially, make meals, and somehow keep the house from looking like a hurricane passed through it.

I know and understand this because my wife and I have gone through this phase of marriage. It's hard to figure out how to find the time or energy to "invest" in one more thing during these busy seasons of life. As a marriage counsellor, I know that offering blanket statements like telling people to invest in their marriage, can often discourage more than encourage.

So, in a practical sense, what does it actually mean to invest in your marriage when life is crazy and beyond? Here are a few bite-sized things to consider doing as a way to invest in your marriage:

Connect Spiritually

One of the most beautiful aspects of marriage comes with the opportunity to emotionally and spiritually connect with another human being. Add to that, the gift of Christian marriage that gives us an opportunity to connect, not only with one another, but with a holy and almighty God.

Oftentimes, believing couples tend to take their spiritual connection for granted, forgetting that some of the most intimate moments in marriage are when we're sharing our hearts, communicating what's in our spirit, and interacting about our relationship with God.

I can honestly tell you that some of the most intimate times I spend with my wife are the moments we sit, hand in hand, at the end of the day and just pray about whatever is going on in our lives. It's a simple act, yet has a supernatural outcome. If you're looking for a really powerful way of investing in your marriage, consider setting some time aside weekly or even daily to pray together and share about what God is doing in each of your lives.

Communicate Regularly

Believe it or not, the average married couple spends just minutes a day in active and meaningful communication. It's also a known fact that communication gets less and less with each year of marriage. I don't know about you, but hearing that saddens me, because there is so much joy in being able to communicate with your spouse.

When it comes to communicating, it's important to realise that there are levels of conversation. Facts are the most superficial level, followed by opinions and ideas, followed by the deepest level of sharing our feelings and emotions with one another. That can be uncomfortable for some people, depending on how they were raised or the kind of communication they've grown accustomed to.

But the truth is, each level of conversation is important, and has to be deliberately worked into conversation. If you want to do something small that will have a big impact on your marriage, set aside 10-20 minutes a day sitting face to face with your spouse, for the sole purpose of communicating. Don't let this be the time to discuss conflict or problems, but just a time to catch up and keep up with one another.

For example, consider asking open ended questions like! What was the best part of your day today? or What's something I can do to help you out this week? The goal of this time is to enjoy each other and encourage one another.

Touch Often

Before we had our 3 boys, I remember observing older couples we were attending the same church with, who had children. I noticed that they hardly ever had any physical contact with each other. No hand-holding. No snuggling on the couch. No arms around the shoulder.

Fast forward a few years and a few kids later, and I totally understand the struggle of trying to connect physically with your spouse, all while being pulled in a million different directions. But even during seasons of life when it's hard to come by, I can tell you that physical touch is such an important part of investing in your marriage.

Take inventory of your marriage, and find times (or even schedule times if you have to!) where you can be deliberate about holding hands, kissing often, making love, or even doing something as simple as touching your spouse's back as you pass them in the kitchen. Physical touch conveys to your spouse that: I notice you, I desire you, and I want to be near you. Talk about a great investment!

Confess and Forgive Frequently

As much as we talk about confession and forgiveness within the church, I believe we often fail to apply it in the context of our marriages, because let's be honest, it's a hard task! The idea of being vulnerable and sharing your weaknesses and shortcomings with another person can be a really hard pill to swallow…which is precisely why God calls us to do it.

The practice of letting down our pride in the act of confession opens the door for the opportunity to forgive, which is the sacred glue that holds marriages together. *The couples I know who are highly satisfied in marriage, are not the ones who have the least amount of disagreement, but the ones who have the most forgiveness.*

God has forgiven each one of us of so much, and those who live in that freedom are freed to forgive others. Invest in your marriage by taking the time to search your heart frequently, being honest with your spouse about the things you are longing to change and the areas you need to ask for forgiveness.

"Get Away" Weekly

They say that couples who "pray together stay together". But I think it can also be said that couples who play together, have the most fun! Life can get busy, and the stress of it all can make us lose sight of the fact that God wants us to enjoy one another and the life he's given us.

Invest in your marriage by taking one time a week and setting aside the time to go out (or stay in if you can't afford a weekly sitter) and do something fun! Play a board game on the living room floor, go out for a fun dinner, take a hike, pack a picnic lunch, or even go on a scenic drive.

Let me remind you that the possibilities are endless and what you're doing matters so much less than who you're doing it with. Rekindle your love for one another, by rekindling your friendship.

Investing in your marriage often means doing small things deliberately that will ultimately have a huge impact. Whether you've been married for 5 days, or 50 years, it's never too early or too late to start making a difference in your marriage.

Chapter 25
Generosity

We all know that the word Generosity needs no introduction. Usually, it's attached to some form of financial capability. How much money do we give to charity? Do we pick up the tab when out with friends? How much money do we drop in the homeless man's bucket? However, the fact that generosity encompasses more than finance is not lost on those in love.

I believe that strong marriages are built by generous people. But there are times when we tend to limit our generosity. Telling you to be generous when things are all good with you and your mate is easy. But what about the times when life, and your spouse, rub you the wrong way?

Generosity in Marriage

May I let you know that there are ways to out give your Spouse When you're too tired to take another step, be generous. Even though you're upset, be generous. As temperatures rise in the bedroom, be generous. So, yes. When times are good, generosity overflows. It's easy to bring flowers home when there's money in the bank. Serving breakfast in bed is no big deal after a good night's rest.

The truth that you and I know is that when our spouse is showering us with praise, it's easy to shower them with love. But a marriage rich in generosity goes beyond the good times. In fact, those muscles are stretched when things get tough and we still choose to give.

Generosity when you're tired, you've had a long day at work and are simply exhausted. All you want to do is go home and chill. You want to stretch your legs, watch your favourite show, and escape the grind. But waiting at home is the person you promised to love for life. When your love is fresh, you can't wait to get home and cuddle with your wife. But familiarity breeds contempt, which is kissing cousins with selfishness.

May I tell you that in order to out give your spouse, you must not let selfishness have a place in your marriage. As difficult as it may be, when you walk through the door, greet your spouse with a kiss. There's nothing like a warm greeting to soothe away the troubles of the day. Offering up a smile and a hug costs nothing.

You may not be able to cook a fancy dinner that night. But a kind and generous spirit will leave your spouse full and your relationship solid. It also opens up an opportunity for enriching and encouraging conversation with your partner.

If the time is right, offer to share your spouse's burden. And, on the flip side, share what's on your heart. Being generous when you're weary may not be easy, but I guarantee it's well worth it. Generosity when you're angry This is a tough one. When you're angry, not only is it selfish, but it's just easier to do stupid stuff and say stupid stuff. It really doesn't matter what it is that made you angry.

It could be something simple, like leaving the toilet seat up. Or it might be something major, like spending the mortgage money on a pair of shoes. Whatever it is, your blood is boiling and you're in no mood to keep your tongue in check. Filtering your words, well, that's for generous folks. And when you're angry, you're in no mood to be generous.

However, if you will allow me to remind you what the Bible say, *"In your anger, do not sin."* When reading that scripture, many people stop there. Generosity, however, reads on. It says, *"do not let the sun go down while you are still angry." (Ephesians 4:26).*

What in the world? Needless to say, all of that is easier said than done. But if you care about your partner, a generous heart helps you do it. Consider the long term ramifications of just flying off the handle. So rather than being ruled by unchecked emotions, allow generosity to cool the fire. You may need to wait an hour or two in order to calm yourself down.

You may need to talk to a friend to get yourself in the right headspace. But once you've done that, let generosity rule the moment. Give your spouse a safe space to share their point of view. I don't want to imply that everything will be resolved right away. But being generous in these moments keeps you from walking your relationship off the cliff.

Generosity in the bedroom Whether times are good or bad in a relationship, chances are, you're having sex. Well, let me put it this way. If times are good, you're making love. If times are bad, you're having sex. In those moments, your main concern is getting your needs met. Interestingly, regardless of how healthy the relationship is, the selfish spouse gets in, gets out, and gets on with life.

Sadly, when intimacy spirals downward, it attempts to take the whole relationship with it. So, what's the fix? Generosity. What gives your wife pleasure? When you're generous, you ensure that her pleasure starts way before you hit the bedroom. What turns your man on? Generosity might mean lingerie and a lap dance.

Truth be told, making love makes relationships strong, plain and simple. Now, I get that every sexual encounter with your spouse won't get the big production. But even the quickie takes forethought and benefits from foreplay. And regardless of where you are, in the bedroom, in the kitchen, or at the office, when the temperatures begin to rise, generosity makes sure your spouse is satisfied…and first.

The best marriages feed off of generous behaviour. But, like anything done well, generosity takes practice. Maybe your marriage needs a fighting chance. Or maybe you're just making deposits to your relationship bank. Whatever the case, be generous with your spouse and have the full, rich union you desire.

DECISION TIME

May I encourage you to accept Jesus Christ as your personal Lord and Saviour today! The Bible say, *"Because if you acknowledge and confess with your lips that Jesus is Lord and in your heart believe (adhere to, trust in, and rely on the truth) that God raised Him from the dead, you will be saved.*

For with the heart a person believes (adhere to, trusts in, and relies on Christ) and so is justified (declared righteous, acceptable to God), and with the mouth he confesses (declares openly and speaks out freely his faith) and confirms (his) salvation." (Romans 10:9-10).

"Lord Jesus, I believe that you died for me and rose again on the third day. I confess that I am a sinner that needs your love and forgiveness. Come into my heart, forgive my sins. I receive your eternal life and confirm your love by giving me peace, joy and supernatural love for other people, in Jesus mighty name" Amen.

OTHER BOOKS BY:

Charles O. Soyoye

Marital Secrets For A Successful Marriage

The Holy Spirit

Marriage, a Miracle of Completion

The Truth Regarding Being Born Again

Available from Amazon and your local bookstore!

Lightning Source UK Ltd.
Milton Keynes UK
UKHW020808211219
355800UK00002B/64/P